D0841000

SPANISH

Pronouns & Prepositions

Frank Nuessel, Ph.D.
University of Louisville
Louisville, Kentucky

All inquiries should be addressed to:
Barron's Educational Series, Inc.
250 Wireless Boulevard
Hauppauge, New York 11788
http://www.barronseduc.com

Library of Congress Catalog Card No. 2006929868

ISBN-13: 978-0-7641-3464-7
ISBN-10: 0-7641-3464-7

Printed in the United States of America

9 8 7 6 5 4 3 2 1

Contents _____

Introduction

Section 1: What Is a Pronoun?

Section 2: What Is a Preposition?

Appendices

Introduction

This book is designed to help you understand pronouns and prepositions in an effortless and enjoyable way. It is an in-depth and comprehensive manual on how to use pronouns and prepositions in sentences. All you need is this book, no matter what stage of learning you find yourself. It can thus be used profitably by:

- Those who know some Spanish, but who wish to improve their knowledge of Spanish grammar in a comprehensive and intensive, but user-friendly way.
- Students enrolled in a Spanish language course in high school, college, or university who feel that they need more practice in Spanish grammar.
- Students enrolled in continuing education classes.
- People anticipating a business or pleasure trip to a Spanish-speaking country.
- Beginners and advanced learners of the language.

If you are a true beginner, you will find that this book makes no assumptions. You will also learn about other aspects of Spanish grammar as you work your way through it. If you are someone who already possesses knowledge of Spanish, you will find this book to be particularly helpful, because it also reviews other aspects of grammar, connecting them to the Spanish pronoun and preposition systems.

You should not skip any chapter, especially if you are a beginner. The book is designed to be sequential and coherent. It builds on grammatical notions and vocabulary introduced in previous chapters. By the end, you will be in a position to grasp the fundamentals of the Spanish pronoun and preposition systems.

PRONOUNS

Section One of this book deals with pronouns in all of their manifestations. The word *pronoun* is a combination of two words. The first part, *pro* is a Latin word that means *in the place of*, whereas the second part of this word refers to *noun*, which is a word that refers to a person, place, or thing. Thus, a pronoun means *in place of a noun*.

For many second-language learners, the pronoun is the part of speech that causes difficulties in acquiring and perfecting mastery of a new language. Section One of this book addresses the different types of pronouns that exist in Spanish, and provides accompanying exercises that allow you to develop a mastery of their usage.

Because a pronoun means in place of a noun, there must be a conversational context so that persons who are speaking know the reference of this part of speech. When you say *I heard it*, the pronoun *it* refers to something that the speaker and the listener know because they have already talked about what *it* is. If neither the speaker nor the hearer know the reference, there is no comprehension—especially if someone new joins in the conversation and that person does not know the reference for the word *it*. When you complete Section One, you will have a thorough knowledge of Spanish pronouns.

PREPOSITIONS

Section Two of this book addresses the part of speech known as a preposition. A preposition is the part of speech that indicates a relationship between other parts of speech such as verbs, nouns, and adjectives. The word preposition literally means something that is "placed before" another word. In this case, a preposition is usually placed before a noun or a noun phrase. This part of speech exists in some form in all languages. It may consist of a single word, or even two or more. Some typical examples in English are *at, to, by, for, next to, in regard to, alongside of,* and so forth. Section Two in this book will help you to understand prepositions in a step-by-step fashion, giving you a full explanation on the usage of this part of speech in Spanish.

An introductory *Pronunciation and Spelling Guide* that explains the basics of Spanish pronunciation and orthography is also provided for your easy reference.

¡Diviértete! *Have fun!*

How to Use This Book _____

This book is divided into two sections. Section One deals with pronouns and it consists of twelve chapters. Each chapter consists of an explanation and exemplification of the pronoun for that particular chapter. Section Two addresses prepositions and it contains three chapters. Again, each chapter contains explanations and exercises on prepositions that will help you to understand their uses and functions.

In the introductory portions of the chapters of Section One and Section Two, you are given all of the information you will need on how to use the pronouns and prepositions under discussion. This discussion is followed by exercises that, although they may appear mechanical, are nevertheless necessary. You cannot use pronouns and prepositions if you do not know the rules that govern their use.

Uses and Features

This section, located at the end of each chapter, contains a summary of how the pronouns and prepositions may be used in a sentence. This final overview will help you to recall what you have learned in each chapter.

Exercises

A variety of exercises appear in each chapter and in the two review chapters to help you master both pronouns and prepositions. Many of the exercises involve translating from English to Spanish. In this area of grammar, there is no better way to grasp the use of these grammatical forms than by comparing how the two languages express certain notions and concepts (especially if you are a self-learner).

Tips, Notes...

Throughout a chapter, tips on how to use a pronoun or a preposition, notes on aspects of grammar that are relevant to the specific material in each chapter, charts introducing new vocabulary and related matters, and the like are interspersed. This feature will allow you to stay within the confines of this single book. You will not need to resort to other materials. Nothing has been taken for granted!

Pronunciation and Spelling Guide

If you are a beginner and need information on how to pronounce and spell Spanish words, you will find a pronunciation guide immediately following this introduction.

Back Matter

Three appendices contain complete conjugations of selected verbs: (1) Regular -**ar**, -**er**, and -**ir** verbs; (2) one reflexive verb (**lavarse** / *to wash oneself*); and (3) six frequently used irregular verbs (**ser** / *to be*, **estar** / *to be*, **tener** / *to have*, **hacer** / *to do, to make*, **haber** / *to have* (auxiliary verb).

You will find the answers to the exercises of all chapters and the English-Spanish vocabulary the for all of the words that have been used in the exercises in this book.

As you can see, *Spanish Pronouns and Prepositions* is an easy-to-use book, designed according to a self-teaching system that lets you learn effortlessly.

Pronunciation and Spelling Guide

Prior to starting with pronouns and prepositions, it is helpful to review the basic facts of Spanish pronunciation and spelling. This will help you when you pronounce certain exercises out loud. Saying all of the exercises in this book aloud is an important part of using Spanish as a spoken language.

Vowels

The Spanish vowels are **a**, **e**, **i**, **o**, **u**. The Spanish vowels are pronounced as follows:

Letter	Pronunciation	As in ...	Example
a	ah	_bah_	**A**rgentina
e	eh	m_et_	**E**cuador
i	eeh	b_eet_	Las **I**slas Canarias
o	oh	b_oat_	**O**viedo
u	ooh	b_oot_	Los Estados **U**nidos

Pronunciation Tip
To pronounce Spanish vowels correctly, keep your mouth open, especially at the end of a word. Exaggerate this until it becomes automatic.

Diphthongs

Diphthongs are combinations of two vowels. If these combinations consist of a high vowel (**i**, **e**) and a low vowel (**o**, **a**, **u**), they are pronounced as a single syllable unless they bear a graphic accent mark, in which case they are pronounced as two separate syllables. The Spanish diphthongs are pronounced as follows:

Letter	Pronunciation	As in ...	Example
ai, ay	ah-ee	<u>I</u>	Jam<u>ai</u>ca
au	ow	<u>ou</u>t	P<u>au</u>
ei, ey	eh-ee	p<u>ay</u>	S<u>ey</u>chelles
eu	ay-oo	<u>ee-oo</u>	R<u>eu</u>nión
ia	ee-ah	<u>y</u>acht	Alban<u>ia</u>
io	ee-o	<u>yo</u>	Villavic<u>io</u>sa
ie	ee-eh	<u>ye</u>s	S<u>ie</u>rra León
iu	yuw	<u>you</u>	C<u>iu</u>dad Real
oi, oy	oy	t<u>oy</u>	Alc<u>oy</u>
ua	oo-ah	<u>w</u>att	G<u>ua</u>temala
uo	oo-oh	<u>whoa</u>	R<u>uo</u>na
ue	oo-eh	<u>whe</u>re	P<u>ue</u>rto Rico
ui, uy	oo-ee	<u>we</u>	R<u>ui</u>dera

Consonants

The Spanish consonants follow. You should note that the letters *ch* and *ll* no longer have separate entries in dictionaries as they did for many years. Now you must look for them under the letters *c* and *l.* The Spanish consonants are pronounced as follows:

Letter	Pronunciation	As in ...	Example
b	b	*bat*	**B**olivia
c	k	*cat*	**C**osta Rica
c	s	*cement*	Beli**c**e
ch	ch	*check*	**Ch**ile
d	d	*deck*	**D**ominica
f	f	*famous*	**F**ilipinas
g	g	*gas*	**G**uatemala
g	h	*hit*	**G**erona
h	(no sound)	*hour*	**H**onduras
j	h	*hat*	**J**erez de la Frontera
k	k (foreign words only)	*Kate*	**K**enia
l	l	*lake*	**L**a Rioja
ll	y (in this hemisphere)	*yes*	Valla**d**olid
m	m	*mat*	**M**edellín
n	n	*name*	**N**icaragua
ñ	ñ (as the *ny* of *canyon*)	*canyon*	Espa**ñ**a
p	p	*pit*	**P**araguay
q	k	*keep*	**Q**uito
r	r (lightly rolled in the middle of a word and trilled at the beginning)	*Roy*	Pe**r**ú, **R**einaldo
rr	no English equivalent. The double **rr** appears only between vowels, whereas a single **r** at the beginning of a word is sharply trilled	*No English equivalent*	**R**ioja, Torrelaguna
s	s	*sit*	**S**anto Domingo
t	t	*tack*	**T**enerife
v	v	*volt*	**V**enezuela
w	w (foreign words only)	*want*	Bots**w**ana
x	h	*hat*	Mé**x**ico
y	y	*yes*	**Y**epes
z	s (in Spain, it sounds like the *th* of *think.*	*set*	**Z**aragoza

Pronunciation Note		
Just like English, there are different regional pronunciations of certain consonants or consonant combinations in Spanish. Spain and Latin American Spanish have the following differences.		
Consonant	**Spain**	**Latin America**
ll	*ly* (like *million*)	*y* (like *yes*)
z	*th* (like *think*)	*s* (like *six*)
c (before *i*, *e*)	*th* (like *think*)	*s* (like *six*)

Spelling

Spanish has the advantage of having very consistent spelling. The following examples show how certain sounds are spelled. In general, these sounds have one spelling before the vowels **a**, **o**, **u** and another before the vowels **e** and **i**. The examples are place names in Spanish-speaking countries. It should be noted that in certain verb verbs tenses (the preterit, the present subjunctive), these rules will be very useful to know.

Letters	Sound	Before a, o, u	Before e, i
c	k	Cartagena Córdoba Cuba	
qu	k		Querétaro Quito
g	g	Galápagos Godelleta Gudiña	
gu	g		Guernica Guinea
z	s	Zarzuela del Monte Zorita	
c	s		Cerezo Cifuentes
j	h	Jalón Badajoz Jumilla	

Written Accents

Spanish has three written accents: (1) the acute accent ´; (2) the tilde ˜; and (3) the dieresis ¨.

   No written stress mark is necessary when a word in Spanish conforms to the following basic rules. We have indicated the stressed syllable with an underline.

Word ends in a vowel, <u>n</u> or <u>s</u>, stress falls on the next to the last syllable	Word ends in a consonant other than <u>n</u> or <u>s</u>, stress falls on the last syllable
Ch<u>i</u>le	Singap<u>u</u>r
C<u>o</u>sta R<u>i</u>ca	Trinid<u>a</u>d
San Mar<u>i</u>no	Portug<u>a</u>l
Las <u>I</u>slas Bah<u>a</u>mas	

   The acute accent is used to indicate that words do not follow the normal stress assignment noted above, e.g., **Japón** / *Japan*, **Panamá** / *Panama*. It is used to indicate that two vowels which are usually a diphthong are to be pronounced separately, e.g., **Turquía** / *Turkey*. It is also used to distinguish identical words, e.g., **solo** / *alone* and **sólo** / *only*, **si** / *if* and **sí** / *yes*, **tu** / *your* and **tú** / *you*, **de** / *of* and **¡dé!** / *give!*.

   The tilde is used for the letter **ñ**, e.g., **España** / *Spain*. The dieresis is used to indicate that the vowel **u** is to be pronounced after the letter **g**, e.g., **bilingüe** / *bilingual*.

   Interrogative words bear a graphic accent.

Interrogative Words	
¿cuál?	*which (one)?*
¿cuáles?	*which (ones)?*
¿cuándo?	*when?*
¿cuánto/-a?	*how much?*
¿cuántos/-as?	*how many?*
¿dónde?	*where?*
¿por qué?	*why?*
¿qué?	*what?*
¿quién?	*who? (one person)*
¿quiénes?	*who? (more than one person)*

The Spanish Alphabet and the Revision of Alphabetizing

On April 27, 1994, the Association of Spanish Language Academies convened in Madrid. It decided to eliminate **CH** and **LL** as separate letters of the Spanish alphabet. Prior to this decision, these letters had separate dictionary entries. Now, however, they appear alphabetically under the letters **C** and **L**, respectively. Likewise, words with the **Ñ** appear in the alphabet together with words that do not contain a tilde (**N**). In this instance, words with **ñ** no longer appear in the dictionary after all words with **n**. The result is that the word **añadir** / *to add* appears before the word **andar** / *to walk*. These changes are noteworthy because older dictionaries do not follow this new system, and you might experience difficulties in locating a particular word.

Section 1 _____

WHAT IS A PRONOUN?

The word *pronoun* consists of two parts: (1) "*pro*" which is from the Latin word meaning *in the place of,* and (2) *noun* which in traditional grammatical terms is a word that refers to a person, place, or thing. A pronoun is just that—a word that stands in the place of a noun. In this sense, a pronoun is a reduced form of "noun phrase" which is a noun and its modifiers (definite and indefinite articles and limiting and descriptive adjectives). Pronouns allow us to refer to other parts of a sentence and to other parts of a discourse between people, i.e., they allow us to refer to persons, places, and things without repeating the entire noun phrase because this is a very efficient way of communicating.

Consider the following sentences.

I read <u>the interesting book</u>.

I read <u>it</u>.

The word *it* is a direct object pronoun that replaces the noun phrase *the interesting book.* In this book, you will learn about the process of changing a noun phrase into a pronoun in a step-by-step process.

Pronouns are very useful grammatical forms, as we have noted, because they allow us to abbreviate our oral and written communication. Imagine if you had to repeat a complete noun phrase every time you were speaking or writing. Consider the following paragraph without pronouns. The pertinent noun phrases are underlined. It has 66 words.

<u>The tall man</u> entered <u>the big room</u>. When I saw <u>the tall man</u> enter <u>the big room</u>, I asked <u>the tall man</u> a question. <u>The tall man</u> then answered me and then <u>the tall man</u> approached <u>the red-haired woman seated in a chair</u>. <u>The red-haired woman seated in the chair</u> saw <u>the tall man</u>, and <u>the red-haired woman seated in the chair</u> recognized <u>the tall man</u>.

Now consider the same paragraph with appropriate pronouns in place of the underlined noun phrases. It has only 40 words. This makes the sentence less tedious and less time-consuming.

<u>The tall man</u> entered <u>the big room</u>. When I saw <u>him</u> enter <u>it</u>, I asked <u>him</u> a question. <u>He</u> then answered me and then <u>he</u> approached <u>the red-haired woman seated in a chair</u>. <u>She</u> saw <u>him</u>, and <u>she</u> recognized <u>him</u>.

Clearly, the second version is much less tiresome, and it is easier to understand. If our communication did not use pronouns, we would be engaged in intolerably long interchanges. For this reason, every language has pronouns. They are an efficient way to speak and interact with other people in speech and in writing.

This book will look at the following twelve types of pronouns:

1. Subject pronouns.
2. Interrogative pronouns (question words).
3. Prepositional pronouns.
4. Direct object pronouns.
5. Indirect object pronouns.
6. Double object pronouns.
7. Reflexive pronouns.
8. Uses of *se.*
9. Possessive pronouns.
10. Demonstrative pronouns.
11. Adjectives as pronouns.
12. Relative pronouns.

In Section 1 of the book you will learn about all of these types of pronouns in a step-by-step process that will enable you to speak and write more clearly in Spanish. There will be many types of notes, tips, and exercises that will allow you to master the various manifestations of pronouns so that when you have completed this manual, you will have an excellent command of the Spanish language.

1

Subject Pronouns

Subject pronouns are words that allow you to talk about yourself, to others, and about others. They may be singular or plural. The following chart illustrates the subject pronouns of Spanish and their corresponding English forms.

	Singular		Plural
1st person	**yo** / *I*	1st person	**nosotros** / *we* (*m.*) **nosotras** / *we* (*f.*)
2nd person	**tú** / *you* (*fam. sg.*)	2nd person	**vosotros** / *you* (*fam. pl. m.*) **vosotras** / *you* (*fam. pl. f.*)
3rd person	**él** / *he* **ella** / *she* **usted** / *you* (*pol. sg.*) **ello** / *it* (*neuter*)	3rd person	**ellos** / *they* (*m.*) **ellas** / *they* (*f.*) **ustedes** / *you* (*pol. pl.*)

While the above chart suggests that there is a very close correspondence between subject pronouns in Spanish and English, there are also some important differences. The following points will help you to understand these differences.

FAMILIAR AND POLITE FORMS OF ADDRESS

As you can see there are both familiar (*fam.*) and polite (*pol.*) forms of address in Spanish. These are **not** to be used alternatively! If you address someone incorrectly, it might be taken as rudeness! So, be careful.

Simply put, the familiar forms are used to address people with whom you are on familiar terms: Members of the family, friends, etc. If you call someone by a first name, then you are obviously on familiar terms.

Remember that the plural (*pl.*) for the singular (*sg.*) form of the familiar (*fam.*) **tú** and the polite form **usted** / *you* <u>in this hemisphere</u> is **ustedes** / *you*. This is the usage that you are most likely to hear unless you are in Spain. In Spain, however, the plural (*pl.*) for **tú** is **vosotros/vosotras** and the plural for **usted** is **ustedes**. In the exercises in this book, we will use the **vosotros/vosotras** forms, but you must remember that they are used only in Spain. The following chart illustrates this point:

Spain:	Singular		Plural
	tú	→	**vosotros, vosostras**
	usted	→	**ustedes**

Latin America: Singular: Plural:

tú	→	**ustedes**
usted	→	**ustedes**

Remember also that **usted** has the following abbreviations: **Ud.** and **Vd.** Likewise, **ustedes** has the following common abbreviations: **Uds.** and **Vds.** In this book, we shall use the abbreviations **Ud.** and **Uds.**

Again, remember that the single English word *you* has many manifestations in Spanish, as illustrated below.

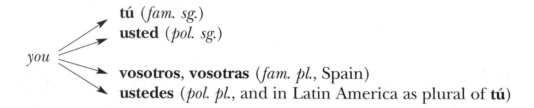

you
- **tú** (*fam. sg.*)
- **usted** (*pol. sg.*)
- **vosotros, vosotras** (*fam. pl.*, Spain)
- **ustedes** (*pol. pl.*, and in Latin America as plural of **tú**)

Grammar Note

Note that there are three pairs of forms of subject pronouns: **nosotros/nosotras** / *we*, **vosotros/vosotras** / *you*, and **ellos/ellas** / *they*. The first form, masculine (*m.*) plural (*pl.*), may refer to men only, or to a group of men and women. The second form, feminine (*f.*) plural (*pl.*), refers only to women.

In this book, we shall abbreviate these forms as **nosotros/-as**, **vosotros/-as**, and **ellos/-as**.

When to Use the Familiar and the Formal Words for You

You will use **Ud.** / *you* (polite singular abbreviated as *pol. sg.*) if you are addressing one person, or **Uds.** / *you* (polite plural; abbreviated as *pol. pl.*) if you are addressing more than one person:

Doctor/-a / *Dr.*
Profesor/-a / *Professor*
Señor / *Mister*
Señora / *Mrs.*
Señorita / *Miss*

Likewise, if you address a person by his or her first name, you will use **tú** / *you* (familiar singular abbreviated as *fam. sg.*). In Spain, if you address a group of peers, you would use **vosotros/-as** / *you* (familiar plural; abbreviated as *fam. pl.*), whereas in this hemisphere, you would use **Uds.** / *you* (*pol. pl.*)

Exercise Set 1-1

Use the appropriate word for the English word *you* (**tú**, **Ud.**, **vosotros**, **vosotras**, **Uds.**) according to the context.

1. Ignacio, _____

2. Profesora Morales, _____

3. Señoras y señores, _____ (Latin America)

4. Isabel y Sonia, _____ (Spain)

5. Estimados colegas, _____ (Spain and Latin America)

Grammar Note

Note that there is no Spanish pronoun for the English word *it*. The pronoun *it* is normally expressed in Spanish by using the third person singular of the verb.

Impersonal expressions follow this grammatical practice, as seen in the following examples:

> **Es cierto.** / *It is certain.*
> **Es posible.** / *It is possible.*
> **Es tarde.** / *It is late.*

Weather expressions also use the third person singular to express the English word *it*:

> **Llueve.** / *It is raining.*
> **Nieva.** / *It is snowing.*
> **Hace sol.** / *It is sunny.*

Time expressions also use the third person singular (or plural) of the verb **ser** / *to be* to express *it*:

> **Es la una de la tarde.** / *It is one P.M.*
> **Son las diez de la noche.** / *It is 10 P.M.*
> **Es el mediodía.** / *It is noon.*

Likewise, *it* may be expressed by the third person singular of the verb **ser** / *to be* in the following cases:

> **Es un coche viejo.** / *It is an old car.*
> **Es de plástico.** / *It is (of) plastic.*
> **Es de Roberto.** / *It is Robert's.*

Because the word *it* appears in the above expressions, English speaking students often place a word in the subject position even though none is called for in Spanish.

Grammar Note
There is a very rarely used third person singular "neuter" subject pronoun that occurs in the following example. **Ello es que no voy.** / _The fact is that I'm not going._

Exercise Set 1-2

Translate the following sentences into Spanish. Be careful about the English word _it_, which is not necessary in Spanish.

1. It is probable.

   _____

2. It is María's (use **de**).

   _____

3. It is raining.

   _____

4. It is 8 p.m.

   _____

5. It is early.

   _____

6. It is metal (use **de**).

   _____

7. It is new.

   _____

8. It is midnight.

   _____

9. It is here.

   _____

10. It is a car.

    _____

SUBJECT PRONOUNS AND SPANISH VERBS

The Spanish verbal system has a set of suffixes, or endings, that indicate the subject of the sentence. To illustrate this point, we provide a set of conjugations for regular verbs in the present indicative, **presente de indicativo**.

The following three verbs are examples of regular verbs of the first conjugation (**hablar** / *to speak*), second conjugation (**beber** / *to drink*), and third conjugation (**vivir** / *to live*). These verbs show the correspondence of the subject pronoun and the verbal ending. They are regular verbs because they follow a predictable pattern in which you add regular endings to the verb stem, which is the verb minus the ending (-**ar**, -**er**, -**ir**).

First Conjugation Verb in the Present Tense

Regular verbs are conjugated in exactly the same manner as other verbs with, of course, the addition of reflexive pronouns immediately before the conjugated verb.

1. Drop the infinitive ending (-**ar**, -**er**, -**ir**). This produces the stem to which you add the verbal endings (see # 2 below).

   <u>habl</u>ar / *to speak* → **habl-**
   <u>beb</u>er / *to drink* → **beb-**
   <u>viv</u>ir / *to live* → **viv-**

2. Add the endings (indicated in bold face type below) to the stem. The following are the endings that you add to the stem of regular -**ar**, **er**, and -**ir** verbs.

Subject Pronoun	Verb Ending (-<u>ar</u>)	Verb Ending (-<u>er</u>)	Verb Ending (-<u>ir</u>)
(yo)	-**o**	-**o**	-**o**
(tú)	-**as**	-**es**	-**es**
(él)	-**a**	-**e**	-**e**
(ella)			
(Ud.)			
(nosotros-/as)	-**amos**	-**emos**	-**imos**
(vosotros/-as)	-**áis**	-**éis**	-**ís**
(ellos/-as)			
(Uds.)	-**an**	-**en**	-**en**

We now provide the conjugation, in the present tense, of a first-conjugation (-**ar**) verb.

hablar / *to speak*

Subject Pronoun	Verb Form	Meaning
(yo)	<u>habl</u> + **o**	*I speak, I am speaking, I do speak*
(tú)	<u>habl</u> + **as**	*you (fam. sg.) speak, you are speaking, you do speak*
(él)	<u>habl</u> + **a**	*he speaks, he is speaking, he does speak*
(ella)	<u>habl</u> + **a**	*she speaks, she is speaking, she does speak*
(Ud.)	<u>habl</u> + **a**	*you (pol. sg.) speak, you are speaking, you do speak*
(nosotros/-as)	<u>habl</u> + **amos**	*we speak, we are speaking, we do speak*
(vosotros/-as)	<u>habl</u> + **áis**	*you (fam. pl.) speak, you are speaking, you do speak*
(ellos)	<u>habl</u> + **an**	*they (m.) speak, they are speaking, they do speak*
(ellas)	<u>habl</u> + **an**	*they (f.) speak, they are speaking, they do speak*
(Uds.)	habl + **an**	*you (pol. pl.) speak, you are speaking, you do speak*

Exercise Set 1-3

Supply the appropriate verbal ending in Spanish for the following **-ar** verbs to correspond with the subject pronoun provided.

1. Yo habl_____

2. Nosotras camin_____

3. Uds. cant_____

4. Tú estudi_____

5. Él bail_____

6. Vosotros toc_____

Second Conjugation Verb in the Present Tense

beber / *to drink*

Subject Pronoun	Verb Form	Meaning
(yo)	<u>beb</u> + **o**	*I drink, I am drinking, I do drink*
(tú)	<u>beb</u> + **es**	*you (fam. sg.) drink, you are drinking, you do drink*
(él)	<u>beb</u> + **e**	*he drinks, he is drinking, he does drink*
(ella)	<u>beb</u> + **e**	*she drinks, she is drinking, she does drink*
(Ud.)	<u>beb</u> + **e**	*you (pol. sg.) drink, you are drinking, you do drink*
(nosotros/-as)	<u>beb</u> + **emos**	*we drink, we are drinking, we do drink*
(vosotros/-as)	<u>beb</u> + **éis**	*you (fam. pl.) drink, you are drinking, you do drink*
(ellos)	<u>beb</u> + **en**	*they (m.) drink, they are drinking, they do drink*
(ellas)	<u>beb</u> + **en**	*they (f.) speak, they are drinking, they do drink*
(Uds.)	<u>beb</u> + **en**	*you (pol. pl.) drink, you are drinking, you do drink*

Exercise Set 1-4

Supply the appropriate verbal ending in Spanish for the following **-er** verbs to correspond with the subject pronoun provided.

1. Tú com_____

2. Vosotras beb_____

3. Nosotros corr_____

4. Ellas le_____

5. Yo vend_____

6. Usted romp_____

Third Conjugation Verb in the Present Tense

vivir / *to live*

Subject Pronoun	Verb Form	Meaning
(yo)	<u>viv</u> + **o**	*I live, I am living, I do live*
(tú)	<u>viv</u> + **es**	*you (fam. sg.) live, you are living, you do live*
(él)	<u>viv</u> + **e**	*he lives, he is living, he does live*
(ella)	<u>viv</u> + **e**	*she lives, she is living, she does live*
(Ud.)	<u>viv</u> + **e**	*you (pol. sg.) live, you are living, you do live*
(nosotros/-as)	<u>viv</u> + **imos**	*we live, we are living, we do live*
(vosotros/-as)	<u>viv</u> + **ís**	*you (fam. pl.) live, you are living, you do live*
(ellos)	<u>viv</u> + **en**	*they (m.) live, they are living, they do live*
(ellas)	<u>viv</u> + **en**	*they (f.) live, they are living, they do live*
(Uds.)	<u>viv</u> + **en**	*you (pol. pl.) live, you are living, you do live*

Exercise Set 1-5

Supply the appropriate verbal ending in Spanish for the following **-ir** verbs to correspond with the subject pronoun provided.

1. Tú viv_____

2. Nosotros abr_____

3. Ella escrib_____

4. Vosotras cubr_____

5. Ellas sufr _____

6. Yo admit_____

Tip

You should note that the following endings, or suffixes, are regularly associated with the following verb forms in Spanish.

Person	Ending
tú	-s*
nosotros/-as	-mos
vosotros/-as	-ís
Uds., ellos/-as	-n

*The preterit tense is the one exception to this rule. It does not have an ending in -s for the **tú** / *you* form.

Usage Notes

Note that the pronouns **yo, tú, nosotros, nosotras, vosotros, vosotras** are normally used to make an emphatic statement.

Observe the difference between the following two sentences:

Hablo español. / *I speak Spanish*. = matter of fact statement.

<u>**Yo**</u> **hablo español**. / <u>*I*</u> *speak Spanish*. = Very emphatic statement (with raised voice in English).

English normally requires a subject pronoun, but in the Spanish verb system the ending tells us who is doing the speaking.

In the third person singular and plural, the subject pronouns are often used because one verb form corresponds to several possible subjects in Spanish:

<u>**Él**</u> **habl<u>a</u>**. / *He speaks*
<u>**Ella**</u> **habl<u>a</u>**. / *She speaks*
<u>**Ud**</u>. **habl<u>a</u>**. / *You (pol. sg.) speak*
<u>**Ellos**</u> **habl<u>an</u>**. / *They (men, or men and women) speak*
<u>**Ellas**</u> **habl<u>an</u>**. / *They (women only) speak*
<u>**Uds**</u>. **habl<u>an</u>**. / *You (pol. pl. in this hemisphere, also plural of the familiar form tú) speak*

In Spanish the **-s** form of the verb corresponds to **tú** / *you* (*fam. sg.*). In English the **-s** form of the verb of the present tense signifies the third person singular:

Spanish:
Tú habla<u>s</u>. / *You speak*.
Él habla. / *He speak<u>s</u>*.

In Spanish, when you include yourself (**yo**) and at least one other person, you must use the **-mos** form of the verb.

> **Javier y yo hablamos español.** / *Javier and I speak Spanish.*
> **Amparo, Enrique y yo hablamos inglés.** / *Amparo, Enrique, and I speak English.*

FAMILIAR AND POLITE FORMS OF ADDRESS WITH VERBS

Remember that in the singular, the **tú** / *you* (familiar singular; abbreviated as *fam. sg.*) forms are used for familiar address (this verb form ends in **-s**), and the **usted** / *you* (polite singular; abbreviated as *pol. sg.*) form for polite address this (this verb form corresponds to the third person singular). Also, recall that **usted** / *you* (*pol. sg.*) has two common abbreviations: **Ud.** and **Vd.** Remember that we shall use **Ud.** in this book.

> **¿Qué necesitas?** / *What do you (fam. sg.) need?*
> **¿Qué necesita Ud.?** / *What do you (pol. sg.) need?*

The **ustedes** form which requires the third person plural form of the verb is used for the plural of both **tú** and **usted** in this hemisphere as noted above. Thus, in this hemisphere, the **ustedes** form (abbreviated as **Uds.** or **Vds.**) is the only plural form for both **tú** and **usted**. Remember that we shall use **Uds.** in this book.

> **¿Miran Uds la televisión?** / *Are you watching TV?*
> **¿Dónde viven Uds.?** / *Where do you live?*

In Spain, the plural of **tú** is **vosotros** (all men or a group of men and women) or **vosotras** (all women). This usage is thus more geographically limited in its usage.

> **¿Habláis español mucho?** / *Do you speak Spanish a lot?*
> **¿Necesitáis estudiar español mucho?** / *Do you need to study Spanish a lot?*

Exercise Set 1-6

A. Supply the appropriate subject pronoun in Spanish for the following present tense **-ar**, **-er**, and **-ir** verbs according to their ending. In some cases, you may be able to use more than one subject pronoun. Remember that you can determine the person (first, second, third, singular and plural) of the verb by its ending.

1. _____ hablamos

2. _____ como

3. _____ vivís

4. _____ habla

5. _____ com<u>en</u>

6. _____ viv<u>e</u>

7. _____ cant<u>amos</u>

8. _____ beb<u>es</u>

9. _____ escrib<u>en</u>

10. _____ compr<u>a</u>

11. _____ corr<u>emos</u>

12. _____ estudi<u>áis</u>

13. _____ comprend<u>e</u>

14. _____ recib<u>o</u>

B. Supply the appropriate subject pronoun (**tú**, **vosotros/-as**, **Ud**. or **Uds**.) according to the context.

1. Dra. Martínez, _____

2. Héctor, _____

3. Rosa y Teresa (this hemisphere), _____

4. Ricardo y Gloria (this hemisphere), _____

5. Señoras y señores, _____

6. Claudio y Manolo (Spain), _____

7. Profesor Ramírez, _____

8. Señores González, _____

Exercise Set 1-7
Translate the following sentences into Spanish.

1. Jorge, you eat here.

_____

2. Marta and Elena, you (Spain) write the letter.

_____

3. Mr. and Mrs. Rodríguez, you (this hemisphere) sing well.

_____

4. Professor Smith, you speak Spanish well.

_____

5. Juan and I work hard.

_____

6. It is late.

_____

7. It is one o'clock.

_____

8. It is two o'clock.

_____

9. We speak Spanish.

_____

10. She lives here.

_____

USES AND FEATURES

Spanish subject pronouns correspond closely to their English counterparts, but there are several points that you will want to recall when you use them.

1. The subject pronouns **yo** / _I_, **tú** / _you_ (_fam. sg._), **nosotros/-as** / _we_, **vosotros/-as** / _you_ (_fam. pl._) are only used with verbs when you want to be emphatic. Since the suffixes, or verbal endings, identify the person and number, it is not necessary to use these forms.

2. The subject pronouns **él** / _he_, **ella** / _she_, **Ud.** / _you_ (_pol. sg._), **ellos** / _they_ (_m._), **ellas** / _they_ (_f._), **Uds.** / _you_ (_pol. pl._) are often used with verbs because the verb forms (third person singular and plural) they are associated with are ambiguous, that is, these verb forms may have more than one reference.

3. Familiar **tú** / _you_, **vosotros/-as** / _you_ (in Spain) and polite forms (**Ud.** / _you_, **Uds.** / _you_) constitute extremely important social distinctions in Spanish. Failure to use these subject pronouns correctly can result in serious communication problems by appearing rude and impolite.

4. In this hemisphere, the plural of **tú** / _you_ is **Uds.** / _you_.

5. Spanish expresses the English word _it_ by using the third person singular of the verb, e.g., **es claro** / _it is clear_; **es la una y media** / _it is one thirty_; **hace viento** / _it is windy_.

Interrogative Pronouns

An interrogative pronoun is one that asks a question. These pronouns may ask questions such as, Who did something? What did someone do? Who(m) did you see? Whose is it?

The following is a list of interrogative pronouns. Note that all of these interrogative pronouns use an upside down question mark (¿) at the beginning. Note also that they all bear a graphic accent mark (´).

Interrogative Pronoun	Meaning
¿quién? *(sg.)*	*who? (sg.)*
¿quiénes? *(pl.)*	*who? (pl.)*
¿qué?	*what?*
¿cuál? *(sg.)*	*which one? (sg.)*
¿cuáles? *(pl.)*	*which ones? (pl.)*

INTERROGATIVE PRONOUNS

Interrogative pronouns seek to answer the question *who?* or *what?* The following sentences illustrate the use of *who?*

¿Quién es? / *Who is it?* (one person)
¿Quiénes son? / *Who are they?* (two or more people)

Exercise Set 2-1

Translate the following sentences into Spanish.

1. Who is she?

   _____

2. Who are the men?

   _____

3. Who is he?

   _____

4. Who are you (*pol. pl.*)?

   _____

¿A quién? and ¿A quiénes?

Except in very formal circumstances in English, we rarely use the word *whom?* when we are asking a question about a direct object that refers to a person (see the following sentence).

> I see Robert.
> *Who(m.) do you see?*

In Spanish, however, there is a special word that indicates that a word or a phrase is a direct object that refers to a person. It is called the *personal a*. It is sometimes called a *function* word, and it indicates that the word that follows is a direct object that refers to a person (see illustrated below). It is a word that is not translated into English but it is very important in Spanish. We have indicated the personal **a** with an underline. When you want to say "whom" in Spanish, this function word must precede **¿quién?** (*sg.*) or **¿quiénes?** (*pl.*) as follows: **¿a quién?** (*sg.*) and **¿a quiénes?** (*pl.*).

> **¿A quién ves?** / *Who(m) do you see?* (one person = *sg.*)
> **Veo a Roberto.** / *I see Robert.*

> **¿A quiénes ves?** / *Who(m) do you see?* (two or more people = *pl.*)
> **Veo a mis amigos.** / *I see my friends.*

Exercise Set 2-2

Translate the following sentences into Spanish. We include the use of the **-m** (*whom*) with these interrogative pronouns to signal that they are direct objects of the main verb, which means that you must use the personal **a**.

1. Who(m) (*sg.*) are you (*fam. sg.*) calling?

_____

2. Who(m) (*pl.*) do you (*fam. sg.*) know?

_____

3. Who(m) (*pl.*) do you (*fam. sg.*) want to see?

_____

4. Who(m) (*sg.*) do you (*fam. sg.*) need?

_____

¿De quién? and *¿De quiénes?*

In Spanish, you express the question word *whose?* in one of two ways: **¿de quién?** (*sg.*) or **¿de quiénes?** (*pl.*) as illustrated below.

> **¿De quién es el coche?** / *Whose car is it?* (*sg.*)
> **Es de María.** / *It's Mary's.*

> **¿De quiénes son los juguetes?** / *Whose toys are they?* (*pl.*)
> **Son de mis hermanos.** / *They are my brothers'.*

Remember that there is no *apostrophe s* (**'s**) in Spanish. This is an English construction that does not exist in Spanish.

Exercise Set 2-3

Translate the following sentences into Spanish.

1. Whose (*sg.*) book is it?

_____

2. Whose (*pl.*) house is it?

_____

3. Whose (*sg.*) coffee is it?

_____

4. Whose (*pl.*) letters are they?

_____

Exercise Set 2-4

Translate the following sentences into Spanish. Remember that the English *it* is represented by the third person singular of the verb.

1. Who (*pl.*) are they?

_____

2. Whose (*sg.*) pen is it?

_____

3. Who(m) (*sg.*) are you (*pol. sg.*) looking for?

_____

4. Who is the woman?

_____

5. Who(m) (*pl.*) do you (*fam. sg.*) want see?

_____

6. Whose (*pl.*) car is it?

_____

7. Who (*sg.*) is it?

_____

8. Who(m) (*pl.*) do you (*fam. sg.*) know?

_____

9. Whose (*sg.*) book is it?

_____

10. Who (*sg.*) is here?

_____

11. Who (*sg.*) drinks coffee?

_____

12. Whose (*sg.*) cat is it?

_____

13. Who(m) (*pl.*) are you (*fam. sg.*) calling?

_____

14. Who (*sg.*) has the car?

_____

¿Qué? and ¿Cuál?/¿Cuáles?

In Spanish, there are two words to express the English word *what?* They are used in very specific ways as we shall see.

You use the question word **¿qué?** / *what?* to ask for identification or a definition when followed by the verb **ser** / *to be* (see the first example below). In addition, **¿qué?** asks a question about something not previously mentioned before with verbs other than **ser** / *to be*. It may also be used with an immediately following noun. In this instance, it is an <u>interrogative adjective</u> and **not** an <u>interrogative pronoun</u> (see the second and third examples below). In the second and third examples, you are asking for a choice among various possibilities.

> **¿Qué es una novela?** / Wh*at is a novel?*
> **¿Qué periódico quieres?** / *Which newspaper do you want?*
> **¿Qué libro lees?** / *What book are you reading?*

The singular interrogative pronominal form **¿cuál?** / *which (one)? / what?* is used when the following word is the preposition **de** / *of,* or a verb as shown on the next page. The plural form **¿cuáles?** / *which (ones) / what* functions the same way as illustrated below. The interrogative pronouns **¿cuál?** / *which (one)* **¿cuáles?** / *which (ones)* ask for a selection from a choice of possibilities.

¿Cuál es tu dirección? / *What is your address?* (from all of the possible addresses)
¿Cuál es la capital de Chile? / *What is the capital of Chile?* (from all of the capitals of the world)

¿Cuáles de tus vecinos conoces mejor? / *Which (ones) of your neighbors do you know better?*
¿Cuáles quieres? Quiero estas novelas. / *Which ones do you want? I want these novels.*

Exercise Set 2-5

Write the appropriate question word (**¿qué?, ¿cuál?, ¿cuáles?**) according to the context provided. Then translate the sentences into Spanish.

1. _____ What is your (*fam. sg.*) name?   _____

2. _____ What is it?   _____

3. _____ What color do you (*fam. sg.*) want?   _____

4. _____ Which student is here?   _____

5. _____ What are you (*fam. sg.*) doing?   _____

6. _____ Which ones do you (*fam. sg.*) need?   _____

7. _____ Which of the two do you (*fam. sg.*) want?   _____

8. _____ Which words do you (*fam. sg.*) remember?   _____

9. _____ What day is it today?   _____

10. _____ What is your (*fam. sg.*) address?   _____

Exercise Set 2-6

Translate the following sentences into Spanish. You will need to choose from the following interrogative expressions for your answers: **¿quién?, ¿quiénes?, ¿a quién?, ¿a quiénes?, ¿de quién?, ¿de quiénes?, ¿qué?, ¿cuál?, ¿cuáles?**. Use each pronoun only once.

1. Whose (*sg.*) money is it?

_____

2. Who is he?

_____

3. What is the capital of Spain?

_____

4 Whom (*sg.*) are you (*fam. sg.*) looking at?

_____

5. What is it?

_____

6. Whose (*pl.*) letters are they?

_____

7. Whom (*pl.*) does she see?

_____

8. What are the parts of a computer?

_____

9. Who are your (*fam. sg.*) friends?

_____

USES AND FEATURES

1. The singular form **¿quién?** / *who?* is used to identify the individual who is performing an action. The plural form **¿quiénes?** / *who?* seeks to identify the people (more than one) who are performing an action.

    ¿Quién es? / *Who is it?*
    ¿Quiénes son ellos? / *Who are they?*

2. **¿A quién?** (*sg.*) / *whom?* and **¿a quiénes?** (*pl.*) / *whom?* are used to identify the direct object or the recipient of an action.

    ¿A quién ves? / *Whom do you see?*
    ¿A quiénes invitas? / *Whom are you inviting?*

3. **¿De quién?** (*sg.*) / *whose?* and **¿de quiénes?** (*pl.*) / *whose?* ask about possession.

    ¿De quién es la casa? / Whose house is it?
    ¿De quiénes es el coche? / Whose car is it?

4. **¿Qué?** / *what/which* asks for an identification or definition. It may be used alone or with a following noun. In the latter case, it is an interrogative adjective and it asks for a selection among several items as illustrated by the second example below.

    ¿Qué es esto? / *What is this?*
    ¿Qué película quieres ver? / *What film do you want to see?*

5. **¿Cuál?** (*sg.*) / *which one?* and **¿cuáles?** (*pl.*) / *which ones?* ask for a selection from a group.

    ¿Cuál es tu apellido? / *What is your surname?*
    ¿Cuáles de tus posesiones prefieres más? / *Which of your possessions do you prefer most?*

3

Prepositional Pronouns

Prepositional pronouns are pronouns used after a preposition, hence their name. You will note that, <u>except for</u> **mí** / *me*, and **ti** / *you* (*fam. sg.*), the forms are just like the <u>subject pronouns</u> discussed in Chapter 1. Here are the Spanish pronouns used after a preposition:

	Singular		Plural
1st person	**mí** / *me*	1st person	**nosotros** / *us* (*m.*) **nosotras** / *us* (*f.*)
2nd person	**ti** / *you* (*fam. sg.*)	2nd person	**vosotros** / *you* (*fam. pl., m.*) **vosotras** / *you* (*fam. pl., f.*)
3rd person	**él** / *him* **ella** / *her* **usted (Ud.)** / *you* (*pol. sg.*) **ello** / *it* (*neuter*)	3rd person	**ellos** / *them* (*m.*) **ellas** / *them* (*f.*) **ustedes (Uds.)** / *you* (*pol. pl.*)

The pronoun **ello** / *it*, sometimes called the "neuter" pronoun, is used to refer to a previous idea, a concept, or a complete sentence. The following example illustrates this.

Todo está arruinado y no quiero hablar de <u>ello</u>. / *Everything is ruined and I do not want to talk about <u>it</u>.*

A preposition may be a single word (simple preposition) such as **a** / *to/at*, or **en** / *on*, and so forth. It may also consist of two, three, or even four words (compound preposition) such as **delante de** / *in front of* or **al lado de** / *next to*, and **a la derecha de** / *to the right of*.

SOME COMMON SIMPLE AND COMPOUND PREPOSITIONS

a	*at, on*	**de**	*from, of*
a la derecha de	*to the right of*	**debajo de**	*beneath*
a la izquierda de	*to the left of*	**delante de**	*in front of*
acerca de	*about*	**en**	*on, in*
al lado de	*beside*	**encima de**	*on top of*
cerca de	*near*	**para**	*for*
con	*with*	**por**	*for, by, through, around*

Some examples of prepositional pronouns with simple and compound prepositions follow.

Hay un libro al lado de <u>mí</u>. / *There is a book beside me.*
El regalo es para <u>ti</u>. / *The gift is for you.*
La revista está cerca de <u>Uds.</u> / *The magazine is near you.*
Es de <u>ellos</u>. / *It's theirs.*
Antonio hizo un error y no quiere hablar de <u>ello</u>. / *Antonio made a mistake and he doesn't want to talk about it.*

Exercise Set 3-1

Translate the following sentences into Spanish.

1. The book is near her.

   _____

2. She is in front of me.

   _____

3. The car is for (**para**) you (*fam. sg.*).

   _____

4. The book is beside you (*pol. sg.*)

   _____

5. The gift is for (**para**) you (*fam. pl., m.*, Spain).

   _____

6. They (*m.*) live to the right of us (*m.*).

   _____

7. The book is hers (*of her*).

   _____

8. He is with you (*pol. pl.*)

   _____

9. She is to the left of you (*fam. sg.*)

   _____

10. They are in front of her.

    _____

Six Exceptional Prepositions

The following six prepositions take a subject pronoun rather than an object pronoun.

entre	*between*	**menos**	*except*
excepto	*except*	**salvo**	*except*
incluso	*including*	**según**	*according to*

When you use these prepositions, you must note the following exceptional usage.

entre tú y yo / *between you and me*
según yo / *according to me*
según tú / *according to you*
excepto yo / *except me*
salvo tú / *except you*
menos yo / *except me*
incluso tú / *including you*

Exercise Set 3-2

Translate the following phrases into Spanish.

1. except me

   _____

2. except you (*fam. sg.*)

   _____

3. according to me

   _____

4. between you (*fam. sg.*) and me

   _____

Exercise Set 3-3

Translate the following sentences into Spanish.

1. I have a book for you (*fam. sg.*).

   _____

2. They (*m.*) are in front of me.

   _____

3. We are beside them (*f.*).

   _____

4. They (*m.*) live near you (*pol. pl*).

   _____

5. The gift is from him.

   _____

6. The bookstore is in front of us (*m.*).

_____

7. According to me, she is here.

_____

8. Between you and me, it is possible.

_____

9. It is for you (*fam. pl., f.*)

_____

10. I don't remember and I don't want to talk about it.

_____

11. Everyone, except me, eats pizza.

_____

12. I eat with you (*pol. pl.*).

_____

13. I live near her.

_____

14. They are in front of you (*fam. sg.*).

_____

Prepositional Pronouns with *Con*

The preposition **con** / *with* has some special forms in the first, second, and third person singular and third person plural, as illustrated below.

	Singular		**Plural**
1st person	**conmigo** / *with me*	1st person	**con nosotros** / *with us* (*m.*) **con nosotras** / with us (*f.*)
2nd person	**contigo** / *with you (fam. sg.)*	2nd person	**con vosotros** / *with you* (*fam. pl., m.*) **con vosotras** / *with you* (*fam. pl., f.*)
3rd person	**consigo** / *with him, with her, with you (pol. sg.)* and **con él** / *with him* **con ella** / *with her* **con Ud.** / *with you (pol. sg.)* **con ello** / *with it (neuter)*	3rd person	**consigo** / *with them, with you* (*pol. pl.*) and **con ellos** / *with them* (*m.*) **con ellas** / *with them* (*f.*) **con Uds.** / *with you (pol. pl.)*

In the first and second person singular, you use the forms **conmigo** / *with me,* and **contigo** / *with you.*

> **Esmeralda baila <u>conmigo</u>**. / *Esmeralda is dancing <u>with me</u>.*
> **Voy al concierto <u>contigo</u>**. / *I am going to the concert <u>with you</u>.*

In the third person singular and plural, there are two forms. The form **consigo** / *with him, with her, with you (pol. sg.), with them, with you (pol. pl.)* is used when the reference is to the subject of the sentence:

> **Andrés trae los libros <u>consigo</u>**. / *Andrés brings the books <u>with him</u>.*
> **Elvira y Marta llevan los paquetes <u>consigo</u>**. / *Elvira and Marta carry the packages <u>with them</u>.*

Compare the above sentences with the following (in which the prepositional pronoun does not refer to the subject).

> **Ana y Luis son estudiantes y ella tiene clases <u>con él</u>**. / *Ana and Luis are students and she has classes <u>with him</u>.*

Exercise Set 3-4

Translate the following sentences.

1. He brings the car with him.

_____

2. She comes with me.

_____

3. I dance with her.

_____

4. They (*m.*) go with you (*fam. sg.*).

_____

5. We eat with them (*m.*).

_____

6. She lives with him.

_____

7. They (*m.*) bring the food with them.

_____

8. They (*m.*) speak with you (*pol. sg.*).

_____

Exercise Set 3-5

Translate the following sentences. Use the appropriate prepositional pronouns according to the context.

1. She is going with me.

   _____

2. According to him, it is raining.

   _____

3. As for (**para**) them (*m.*), María sings well.

   _____

4. He always brings his book with him.

   _____

5. They (*m.*) are near me.

   _____

6. He studies with her.

   _____

7. They are for (**para**) you (*fam. sg.*).

   _____

8. Including me, there are three students.

   _____

9. They (*m.*) are with you (*fam. sg.*).

   _____

10. They (*m.*) live next to us (*m.*).

    _____

Uses and Features

1. Prepositional pronouns are used after a simple or a compound preposition.

   Para mí, los pronombres son fáciles. / *As for me, pronouns are easy.*

   Ella está delante de él. / *She is in front of him.*

2. There are six simple prepositions (**entre, excepto, incluso, menos, salvo, según**) that use a subject pronoun rather than an object pronoun.

   incluso yo / *including me*

3. There are some exceptional prepositional forms used with **con** / *with* (**conmigo, contigo, consigo**).

   Ella va conmigo. / *She is going with me.*

4

Direct Object Pronouns

A direct object pronoun substitutes for a direct object. These pronouns are used as objects of verbs, and their placement is different in English and Spanish. For this reason, it is necessary to practice their usage.

Direct objects answer the questions *whom?* or *what?* as shown below.

Whom do you see?
I see **Mary**. **Mary** is the direct object of the sentence.

What do you wear?
I wear **new shoes**. **New shoes** is the direct object of the sentence.

You may substitute direct object pronouns for the direct object, in the preceding sentences as illustrated below.

I see **Mary**.
|
I see **her**.

I wear **new shoes**.
|
I wear **them**.

Here are the Spanish direct object pronouns:

	Singular		**Plural**
1st person	**me** / *me*	1st person	**nos** / *us*
2nd person	**te** / *you (fam. sg.)*	2nd person	**os** / *you (fam. pl.)*
3rd person	**lo** / *him, you (pol. sg., m)* **la** / *her, you (pol. sg., f.)*	3rd person	**los** / *them, you (pol. pl., m.* **las** / *them, you (pol. pl., f.)*

The English third person direct object pronoun *it* (or plural *them*) is expressed by the third person direct object pronoun forms above. Be careful! Choose the pronoun according to the <u>gender</u> and <u>number</u> of the <u>Spanish noun</u> that has been replaced.

The following examples illustrate the process of changing third person direct objects to direct object pronouns (the direct objects and direct object pronouns are underlined). We include examples of masculine and feminine, singular and plural nouns which are then substituted by their corresponding pronouns, that is, those that agree in number (singular, plural) and gender (masculine, feminine) with the noun that they replace. We have underlined the direct object and the corresponding direct object pronouns that replace them in each example sentence.

Concepción lee el periódico. / *Concepción reads the newspaper.* →

Concepción lo lee. / *Concepción reads it.*

Rafael vende los libros. / *Rafael sells the books.* →

Rafael los vende. / *Rafael sells them.*

Berta bebe la leche. / *Berta drinks the milk.* →

Berta la bebe. / *Berta drinks it.*

Jorge compra las revistas. / *Jorge buys the magazines.* →

Jorge las compra. / *Jorge buys them.*

The following chart will help to illustrate the difference in the placement of direct object pronouns between English and Spanish. Notice the placement of the direct object pronouns in each language. In English, the direct object pronoun goes <u>after</u> the verb. In Spanish, the direct object pronoun goes immediately <u>before</u> the conjugated verb.

John sees +
$\left\{ \begin{array}{l} \textbf{me} \\ \textbf{you} \\ \textbf{him, her, it} \\ \textbf{us} \\ \textbf{you} \\ \textbf{them} \end{array} \right.$

Compare this to the Spanish format for the same sentences. In Spanish, the direct object pronoun goes immediately before the conjugated verb.

<u>Juan</u> +
$\left\{ \begin{array}{l} \textbf{me} \\ \textbf{te} \\ \textbf{lo, la} \\ \textbf{nos} \\ \textbf{os} \\ \textbf{los, las} \end{array} \right\}$
+ <u>ve</u>

Exercise Set 4-1

Translate the following sentences. Pay attention to the placement of the direct object pronoun in Spanish.

1. Mario buys them (*books*).

   _____

2. Rosa and Claudio sell it (*car*).

   _____

3. We buy it (*food*) here.

   _____

4. They drink it (*coffee*).

   _____

5. She studies it (*Spanish*).

   _____

6. They see her.

   _____

7. I need them (*books*).

   _____

8. We see them (*cars*).

   _____

9. I sing it (*song*).

   _____

10. I fear him.

   _____

Place of Direct Object Pronouns with Infinitives and Gerunds

The placement of direct object pronouns with respect to the verb follows set patterns. Direct object pronouns must appear immediately before a conjugated verb. The situation is different, however, when there is an <u>infinitive</u> or a <u>present participle</u> (<u>gerund</u>) as shown below. In these cases, the object pronoun may follow and be attached to the infinitive (the form of the verb ending in **-r**), or the present participle (gerund, the form of the verb that ends in **-ndo**), or it may also go immediately before the conjugated verb. You will use them frequently in conversation and in writing, so you need to know how to use them. We have underlined the direct objects and their corresponding direct object pronouns to help you visualize the process. Note that when you add a direct object pronoun to a present participle (gerund), you must write a graphic accent to indicate where the stress originally fell prior to the addition of the pronoun. We have indicated this with italic typeface.

1. **Infinitives**

    Claudia debe comprar <u>el libro</u>. / *Claudia must buy <u>the book</u>.* →
    Claudia debe comprar<u>lo</u>. / *Claudia must buy <u>it</u>.*
    Claudia <u>lo</u> debe comprar. / *Claudia must buy <u>it</u>.*

2. **Present Participles (Gerunds)**

    Claudia está comprando <u>el libro</u>. / *Claudia is buying <u>the book</u>.* →
    Claudia está compr*á*ndo<u>lo</u>. / *Claudia is buying <u>it</u>.*
    Claudia <u>lo</u> está comprando. / *Claudia is buying <u>it</u>.*

Grammar Note

Remember that the negative word **no** / *no, not* goes immediately **before** a verb **unless** there is an object pronoun, in which case **no** goes **before** the object pronoun. See below for examples with a single verb, an infinitive, and a present participle (gerund). We have indicated the negative word in Spanish in italic type.

The order of the negative word **no** and the direct object pronoun is the following:

NO + DIRECT OBJECT + CONJUGATED VERB

Remember, however, that direct object pronouns may optionally follow and be attached to infinitives and present participles (gerunds). In these cases the negative word **no** / *no, not* goes immediately before the verb. We have underlined the direct object and the direct object pronoun.

Claudia *no* compra <u>el libro</u>. / *Claudia is not buying <u>the book</u>.* →
Claudia *no* <u>lo</u> compra. / *Claudia is not buying <u>it</u>.*

Claudia *no* debe comprar <u>el libro</u>. / *Claudia must not buy <u>the book</u>.* →
Claudia *no* debe comprar<u>lo</u>. / *Claudia must not buy <u>it</u>.*
Claudia *no* <u>lo</u> debe comprar. / *Claudia must not buy <u>it</u>.*

Claudia *no* está comprando <u>el libro</u>. / *Claudia is not buying <u>the book</u>.* →
Claudia *no* está compr*á*ndo<u>lo</u>. / *Claudia is not buying <u>it</u>.*
Claudia *no* <u>lo</u> está comprando. / *Claudia is not buying <u>it</u>.*

> ### Grammar Note
>
> If you add a direct object pronoun to a present participle, you must write a graphic accent mark on the place where the stress originally fell to indicate that it is maintained there. We indicate this with italic typeface:
>
> **Estoy haciéndo_lo_.** / *I am doing it.*
> **Estoy escribiéndo_la_**. / *I am writing it.*

Exercise Set 4-2

A. Replace the direct objects with direct object pronouns. Remember that there are two options with infinitives and present participles (gerunds). In such cases, write both possibilities.

> Examples: Alba hace <u>la tarea</u>.
> Alba <u>la</u> hace.
>
> Alba no quiere hacer <u>la tarea</u>.
> Alba no quiere hacer<u>la</u>.
> Alba no <u>la</u> quiere hacer.
>
> Alba está haciendo <u>la tarea</u>.
> Alba está haciéndo<u>la</u>.
> Alba <u>la</u> está haciendo.

1. Aurelio lee <u>las novelas</u>.

_____

2. Esperanza está bebiendo <u>el té</u>.

_____

3. Quieres cantar <u>la canción</u>.

_____

_____

4. Escribo <u>la carta</u>.

_____

5. Ella come <u>los guisantes</u>.

_____

B. Translate the following sentences (*sg.* = singular, *pl.* = plural, *fam.* = familiar, *pol.* = polite). Use a direct object pronoun in your answer. If there are two ways of writing the answer, please do so.

1. I see her here.

_____

2. You (*fam. sg.*) need to watch it (*soap opera*).

_____

_____

3. She is reading (*present participle, gerund*) it (*book*) now.

_____

_____

4. They (*m.*) do not need it (*money*).

_____

5. He sees us.

_____

6. We have them (*books*).

_____

7. They (*m.*) do not need to write it (*composition*).

_____

_____

8. I am not eating it (*pizza*).

_____

_____

9. We see you (*pol. sg., f.*).

_____

10. They (*m.*) want to call her.

_____

_____

C. Answer the following questions. Use a direct object pronoun in your answer. If there are two ways of writing the answer, please do so.

1. ¿Lee Ud. <u>los cuentos</u>?

_____

2. ¿Quieres hacer <u>el trabajo</u> ahora?

_____

_____

3. ¿Están Uds. leyendo <u>el libro de texto</u>?

_____

D. Rewrite the following sentences. Substitute a direct object pronoun for the direct object. Then make the sentence **negative**. Place the negative word **no** / _no, not_ in the appropriate place with respect to the verb. If there are two ways or writing the sentence, write both possibilities.

1. Raúl bebe <u>el café</u>.

_____

2. Salvador y Gloria quieren estudiar <u>la lección</u>.

_____

_____

3. Estoy leyendo <u>la novela</u>.

_____

_____

4. Escribimos <u>la carta</u>.

_____

5. Camilo necesita hacer <u>el trabajo</u>.

_____

_____

USES AND FEATURES

Remember the following points about direct object pronouns.

1. The direct object pronoun goes immediately before a conjugated verb.

    Bebo <u>la leche</u>. / *I drink milk.*
    <u>La</u> bebo. / *I drink it.*

2. The direct object pronoun may follow and be attached to an infinitive or present participle (gerund). Optionally, it may also appear immediately before the conjugated verb. We have underlined the direct object pronouns.

    Voy a comprar<u>lo</u>. / *I am going to buy it.*
    <u>Lo</u> voy a comprar. / *I am going to buy it.*

    Estoy leyéndo<u>lo</u>. / *I am reading it.*
    <u>Lo</u> estoy leyendo. / *I am reading it.*

3. Remember that you add a graphic accent mark when you add a direct object pronoun to a present participle, as illustrated below.

    Estoy comprándo<u>lo</u>. / *I am buying it.*

4. Third person singular and plural direct object pronouns agree in gender (masculine/feminine) and number (singular/plural) with the noun that they substitute.

    Escribo <u>las cartas</u> (*f. pl.*). / *I write the letters.*
    <u>Las</u> escribo. / *I write them.*

    Compro <u>el libro</u>. / I buy the book.
    <u>Lo</u> compro. / *I buy it.*

5. The negative word **no** / *no, not* goes immediately before the direct object pronoun when that pronoun goes before the verb.

    No <u>lo</u> **compro.** / *I'm not buying it.*
    No <u>lo</u> **voy a comprar.** / *I'm not going to buy it.*
    No <u>lo</u> **estoy comprando.** / *I'm not buying it.*

5

Indirect Object Pronouns

Indirect objects normally occur with verbs of communication and verbs of giving and transmitting. Indirect objects answer the questions *to whom?* or *for whom?* illustrated below (the indirect objects are underlined).

To whom are you speaking?
I am speaking **to Mary**.

To Mary is the indirect object.
For whom are you buying the book?

I am buying the book **for Mary**.
For Mary is the indirect object.

The preceding indirect objects may be substituted by indirect object pronouns as illustrated below with underlining.

I am speaking **to Mary**.

I am speaking **to her**.

I am buying the book **for Mary**.

I am buying the book **for her**.

Grammar Note

In some cases in English, there is **no** "to" or "for" phrase to identify the indirect object pronoun, as illustrated below with an underline. In these cases, you must rephrase the sentence (see the second sentence in each example) to uncover the "hidden" indirect object.

I send Paul the money. = I send the money to Paul.
She sells my friends the car. = She sells the car to my friends.

I give him the book. = I give the book to him.
I show them the gift. = I show the gift to them.

Once you learn the pronouns and the rules for their use, you will be able to use them throughout the rest of this book and in your daily communication in Spanish. This is why you are practicing their use now. They are always used in association with verbs, so you need to know how to use them in these situations.

Because the third person singular (**le**) and third person plural (**les**) forms are ambiguous, it is necessary to use clarifying prepositional pronouns (with the preposition **a** / *to/for*) to specify the reference for these two pronominal forms. Review Chapter 3 for the forms and usage of the prepositional pronouns. You will notice that the forms **me**, **te**, **nos**, and **os** are identical to the direct object pronouns. The only formal difference between direct and indirect object pronouns is in the third person singular (**le**) and plural (**les**).

The table with the indirect object pronouns follows.

Singular		Plural	
1st person	**me** / *to/for me*	1st person	**nos** / *to/for us*
2nd person	**te** / *to/for you (fam. sg.)*	2nd person	**os** / *to/for you (fam. pl.)*
3rd person	**le** / *to/for him, to/for her, to/for you (pol. sg.)*	3rd person	**les** / *to/for them, to/for you (pol. pl.)*

Indirect objects normally occur with verbs of communication and verbs of transmission and giving. The following are some common verbs that belong to these categories.

Some Common Verbs of Communication

cantar	*to sing to*	**escribir**	*to write*
contar (ue)	*to tell (a story)*	**gritar**	*to shout*
decir (i)	*to say, to tell*	**hablar**	*to speak*

Some Common Verbs of Transmission and Giving

dar	*to give*	**mostrar (ue)**	*to show*
entregar	*to hand over*	**regalar**	*to give as a gift*
enviar	*to send*	**traer**	*to bring*
mandar	*to send*	**vender**	*to sell*

Placement of Indirect Object Pronouns

Indirect object pronouns appear in the same positions as direct object pronouns, that is, immediately before a conjugated verb as illustrated below.

The following comparisons will help to illustrate the difference in the placement of indirect object pronouns between English and Spanish. In English, the indirect object pronoun goes <u>after</u> the verb. In Spanish, the indirect object pronoun goes immediately <u>before</u> the verb.

$$
\textit{John gives + the book +} \left\{
\begin{array}{l}
\textbf{to me} \\
\textbf{to you} \\
\textbf{to him, to her} \\
\textbf{to us} \\
\textbf{to you} \\
\textbf{to them}
\end{array}
\right.
$$

In English, you may also place the indirect object pronoun before the word *book*. When you do this in English, you do not express the preposition *to* as illustrated below. Again, the indirect object pronoun goes after the verb.

$$
\textit{John gives +} \left\{
\begin{array}{l}
\textbf{me} \\
\textbf{you} \\
\textbf{him, her} \\
\textbf{us} \\
\textbf{you} \\
\textbf{them}
\end{array}
\right\} \textit{ + the book.}
$$

Compare this to the Spanish format for the same sentences. In Spanish, the indirect object pronoun goes immediately before the conjugated verb.

$$
\textbf{Juan +} \left\{
\begin{array}{l}
\textbf{me} \\
\textbf{te} \\
\textbf{le} \\
\textbf{nos} \\
\textbf{os} \\
\textbf{les}
\end{array}
\right\} \textbf{ + da el libro (a él, a ella, a Ud., a ellos, a ellas, a Uds.)}
$$

Redundant Indirect Object Pronoun in Third Person Singular and Plural

It must be remembered that the third person singular (**le**) and plural (**les**) indirect object pronoun must always be used even though it seems unnecessary to English speakers. For this reason, they are called "redundant indirect object pronouns." You will also note that the examples include prepositional pronouns (those that are used after a preposition; see Chapter 3). We have underlined the indirect object pronouns and their corresponding indirect object prepositional phrases to help you see more clearly their placement with respect to the verbs. You will note that in every one of these cases, the indirect object prepositional phrase serves to clarify the indirect object pronoun that is ambiguous, that is, it could refer to any of the following if not clarified: **a él** / *to him,* **a ella** / *to her,* **a usted** / *to you* (*pol. sg.*), **a ellos** / *to them,* **a ellas** / *to them* (all women), **a ustedes** / *to you* (*pol. pl.*).

1. Conjugated verb.

   Le doy el libro a él. / *I give the book to him.*

2. Infinitive.

   Quiero decirle la verdad a ella. / *I want to tell the truth to her.*

   Le quiero decir la verdad a ella. / *I want to tell the truth to her.*

3. Present participle (gerund).

   Estoy mandádoles el paquete a ellos. / *I am sending the package to them.*

   Les estoy mandando el paquete a ellos. / *I am sending the package to them.*

This redundancy becomes even more obvious when you use a specified indirect object, a word or a phrase that refers to a person or persons, as illustrated below.

1. Conjugated verb.

   Le doy el libro a Eva. / *I give the book to Eva.*

2. Infinitive.

Quiero decirle la verdad a Eva. / *I want to tell the truth to Eva.*

Le quiero decir la verdad a Eva. / *I want to tell the truth to Eva.*

3. Present participle (gerund).

Estoy mandándoles el paquete a amigos. / *I am sending the package to friends.*

Les estoy mandando el paquete a amigos. / *I am sending the package to friends.*

Grammar Note

If you add an indirect object pronoun to a present participle, you must write a graphic accent mark on the place where the stress originally fell to indicate that it is maintained there. We have indicated the location of the graphic accent with italic typeface.

Estoy diciéndole la verdad a ella. / *I am telling the truth to her.*
Estoy escribiéndole la carta a él. / *I am writing the letter to him.*

Exercise Set 5-1

Translate the following sentences. Use an indirect object pronoun in your answer. Remember to use the redundant indirect object pronoun in the third person singular and plural. If there are two ways of writing the answer, please do so.

1. I speak to her in Spanish.

_____

2. We give them (*m.*) the pager.

_____

3. They (*m.*) are going to sell us the cell phone.

_____

_____

4. He is sending (*present participle / gerund*) us the email.

_____

_____

Placement of No / *No/Not*

Just like direct object pronouns, indirect object pronouns come immediately before a conjugated verb. If there is a negative word, the order is the following: ***no* + indirect object + conjugated verb**. The following examples illustrate this point. Remember, however, that indirect object pronouns may optionally follow and be attached to <u>infinitives</u> (the form of the verb that ends in **-r**) and <u>present participles</u> (<u>gerunds</u>, the form of the verb that ends in **-ndo**). In these cases the negative word **no** / *no/not* goes immediately before the verb. We have placed the Spanish word **no** in italic typeface. We have also underlined the indirect object pronoun and its corresponding prepositional phrase to help you to visualize their placement.

>*No* <u>le</u> **doy el libro <u>a él</u>.** / *I don't give the book <u>to him</u>.*

>*No* **quiero decir<u>le</u> la verdad <u>a ella</u>.** / *I don't want to tell the truth <u>to her</u>.*

>*No* <u>le</u> **quiero decir la verdad <u>a ella</u>.** / *I don't want to tell the truth <u>to her</u>.*

>*No* **estoy escribiéndo<u>les</u> la carta <u>a ellos</u>.** / *I am not writing the letter <u>to them</u>.*

>*No* <u>les</u> **estoy escribiendo la carta <u>a ellos</u>.** / *I am not writing the letter <u>to them</u>.*

Exercise Set 5-2

Translate the following sentences. Use an indirect object pronoun in your answers. Remember to use the redundant indirect object pronoun in the third person singular and plural. Remember also to place the negative word **no** in the appropriate place with respect to the verb. If there are two ways of writing the answer, please do so.

1. I am not giving him the remote control.

   _____

2. They (*m.*) do not speak to us in English.

   _____

3. They (*m.*) should not show them (*m.*) the video game.

   _____

   _____

4. You (*pol. sg.*) are not sending (*present participle / gerund*) him the organizer.

   _____

   _____

Exercise Set 5-3

A. Translate the following sentences. Use the redundant indirect object pronoun in the third person singular and plural. If there are two ways of writing the answer, do so.

1. I tell the truth to her.

   _____

2. They (*m.*) need to write the letter to them (*m.*).

   _____

   _____

3. They (*m.*) are speaking (*present participle / gerund*) in Spanish to us.

   _____

   _____

4. He must speak to me.

   _____

   _____

5. They (*m.*) do not sell the car to her.

   _____

6. She shows the house to me.

   _____

7. They (*m.*) speak to you (*pol. pl.*)

   _____

8. I am not going to give him the money.

   _____

   _____

B. Answer the following questions. Use the redundant indirect object pronoun in the third person singular and plural. If there are two ways of writing the answer, do so.

1. ¿Le das los libros a Berta?

   _____

2. Prefieres darle los regalos a tu novia?

_____

_____

3. ¿Estás entregándole el paquete a Joaquín?

_____

_____

4. ¿Me vendes el coche?

_____

5. ¿Nos habla Ud. en español?

_____

The Verb *Gustar* / *to be pleasing to, to like*

The verb **gustar** / *to be pleasing to, to like* is another important and very common verb. Its present indicative forms are given below. Its formation is regular, but its usage is different from the English verb *to like*. **Gustar** / *to like* is almost always used in the third person singular or plural because of its special usage and basic meaning of *to be pleasing to*.

gustar / *to be pleasing to, to like*

Subject Pronoun	Verb Form	Meaning
(yo)	gust+**o**	*I am pleasing to*
(tú)	gust+**as**	*you (fam. sg.) are pleasing to*
(él, ,ella, Ud.)	gust+**a**	*he, she, you (pol. sg.) is/are pleasing to*
(nosotros-/as)	gust+**amos**	*we are pleasing to*
(vosotros/-as)	gust+**áis**	*you (fam. pl.) are pleasing to*
(ellos/-as, Uds.)	gust+**an**	*they, you (pol. pl.) are pleasing to*

This verb allows you to express what you *like* in Spanish. It is, however, a tricky verb because it really means *to be pleasing to*.

1. The best initial learning strategy is to rephrase the English expression in your mind as shown below. Notice that the indirect object pronouns precede the verb. We have underlined the indirect object pronouns in Spanish.

English Expression	*Rephrase to*	*Spanish Expression*
↓	↓	↓
I like the novel.	"To me is pleasing the novel."	<u>**Me**</u> **gusta la novela.**
We like the magazines.	"To us are pleasing the magazines."	<u>**Nos**</u> **gustan las revistas.**

2. If the indirect object is not a pronoun, use the preposition **a** before it. Note that when you are talking about someone, you will also need to use the indirect object pronoun **le** or **les**. We have underlined the indirect objects and indirect object pronouns in Spanish.

English Expression	Rephrase to	Spanish Expression
↓	↓	↓
Elena likes the novel.	"To Elena is pleasing the novel."	**<u>A Elena</u> <u>le</u> gusta la novela.**
My friends like the novels.	"To my friends are pleasing the novels."	**<u>A mis amigos</u> <u>les</u> gustan las novelas.**

Note

When **gustar** is used with persons, it means, *I am attracted to.* If you want to say "I like someone," you need to use the expression **caer bien a** / *to like*. The following examples show this usage.

> **<u>Me</u> caes bien.** / *I like you.*

Compare the above usage to the **gustar** expression with a person.

> **<u>Me</u> gustas.** / *I am attracted to you.*

Prepositional Pronouns with *Gustar / to be pleasing to*

You need to review the prepositional pronouns (see Chapter 3). These pronouns, used after prepositions, are especially useful for the **gustar**-type verbs discussed above. Prepositional pronouns are often used with third person singular (**le**) and third person plural (**les**) indirect object pronouns to clarify ambiguous forms that may mean *to him, to her, to you* (*pol. sg.*), *to them* (*m.* or *f.*), and *to you* (*pol. pl.*).

Grammar Note

If you use a third person indirect pronoun, you will need to include a clarifying pronominal phrase as shown below. The clarifying phrase and the indirect object pronoun are underlined.

> **<u>A él</u> <u>le</u> gusta la casa.** / *He likes the house.*
> **<u>A ella</u> <u>le</u> gusta la casa.** / *She likes the house.*
> **<u>A Ud.</u> <u>le</u> gusta la casa.** / *You like the house.*
> **<u>A ellos</u> <u>les</u> gusta la casa.** / *They like the house.*
> **<u>A ellas</u> <u>les</u> gusta la casa.** / *They like the house.*
> **<u>A Uds.</u> <u>les</u> gusta la casa.** / *You like the house.*

Remember that if you use an indirect object (word or phrase), you also use an indirect object pronoun in the sentence:

> **A Antonio le gusta leer.** / *Antonio likes to read.*
> **A mis padres les gustan las matemáticas.** / *My parents like math.*

You may use the first- and second-person singular and plural prepositional objects with **gustar**-type constructions to achieve greater emphasis:

> **Me gusta leer libros.** / *I like to read books.* (ordinary statement)
> **A mí me gusta leer libros.** / *I like to read books.* (very emphatic statement)
>
> **Nos gusta Santiago.** / *We like Santiago.* (ordinary statement)
> **A nosotros nos gusta Santiago.** / *We like Santiago.* (very emphatic statement)

Gustar in Affirmative Statements

As you can see, **gustar** can be confusing for anyone accustomed to the English verb *to like*. The following rule of thumb might help you to use this important verb more easily.

Since the verb is often used with indirect object pronouns, just think of the pronouns as subjects; then make the verb agree with the direct object.

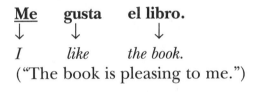

("The book is pleasing to me.")

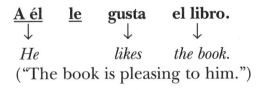

("The books are pleasing to you.")

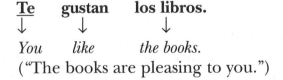

("The book is pleasing to him.")

A ella **le** **gusta** **el libro.**
  ↓   ↓   ↓   ↓
 She   *likes*   *the book.*
("The book is pleasing to her.")

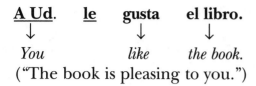

A Ud.   **le**   **gusta**   **el libro.**

You   *like*   *the book.*

("The book is pleasing to you.")

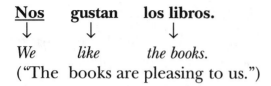

Nos   **gustan**   **los libros.**

We   *like*   *the books.*

("The books are pleasing to us.")

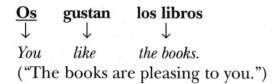

Os   **gustan**   **los libros**

You   *like*   *the books.*

("The books are pleasing to you.")

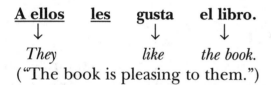

A ellos   **les**   **gusta**   **el libro.**

They   *like*   *the book.*

("The book is pleasing to them.")

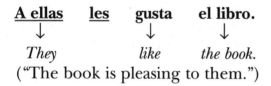

A ellas   **les**   **gusta**   **el libro.**

They   *like*   *the book.*

("The book is pleasing to them.")

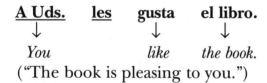

A Uds.   **les**   **gusta**   **el libro.**

You   *like*   *the book.*

("The book is pleasing to you.")

Remember that this is just a rule of thumb. If you are unsure, you must review the text connected with **gustar** in its entirety. Remember also that in the third person singular and plural, you use a prepositional pronoun phrase and indirect object to indicate *what* is pleasing *to whom*.

Exercise Set 5-4

Rephrase each sentence as shown, and then give its Spanish equivalent.

> *Example:* I like the book.
> "The book is pleasing to me." → *Me gusta el libro.*

1. I like the books.

   _____

2. My friends like the restaurant.

   _____

3. You (*fam. sg.*) like to watch soap operas.

   _____

4. She likes the car.

   _____

5. They (*m.*) like the magazines.

   _____

6. Do you (*pol. sg.*) like the food?

   _____

7. I am attracted to you (*fam. sg.*).

   _____

8. I like you (*fam. sg.*).

   _____

9. You (*pol. pl.*) like to swim in the sea.

   _____

10. We like to sing.

    _____

Note

If you want to make a **gustar** construction negative, you must place the word **no** <u>immediately before</u> the indirect object pronoun:

> *No* <u>me</u> **gustan los libros.** / *I do not like the books.*
> **A mí** *no* **me gustan los libros.** / *I don't like the books.*
> **A ella** *no* <u>le</u> **gusta la casa.** / *She doesn't like the house.*

Exercise Set 5-5

Rephrase each sentence as shown, and then give its Spanish equivalent.

> *Example:* I do not like the book.
> "The book is not pleasing to me." → *No me gusta el libro.*

1. I do not like the books.

_____

2. We do not like the headphones.

_____

3. You (*fam. sg.*) do not like the battery charger.

_____

4. He does not like the program.

_____

5. They (*m.*) do not like the CD.

_____

Other Verbs with *Gustar* Features

The following verbs exhibit the same grammatical behavior of **gustar** / *to be pleasing to*—that is, they require frequent usage of indirect object pronouns and they may be rephrased mentally in analogous ways.

Verbs That Function Like *Gustar* / *to be pleasing to*

agradar	*to please*
apetecer	*to be appetizing, to appeal to (food)*
bastar	*to be sufficient, to be enough*
caer bien	*to be liked, to create a good impression*
convenir (ie)	*to suit one's interest, to be good for*
doler (ue)	*to be painful, to ache*
encantar	*to be enchanting to*
faltar	*to be lacking to, to be missing to*
fascinar	*to be fascinating to*
importar	*to be important to*
interesar	*to be interesting to*
molestar	*to bother, to annoy*
parecer	*to seem, to appear to*
sobrar	*to remain, to be left over*

Exercise Set 5-6

A. The following exercise contains verbs that function like **gustar**. Rephrase each sentence as shown, and then give its Spanish equivalent.

    Example: I am interested in the book.
              "The book is interesting to me." → *Me interesa el libro.*

  1. Her tooth aches.

    _____

  2. I lack twenty euros.

    _____

  3. I am not interested in books.

    _____

  4. Foolish people bother him.

    _____

  5. It suits your (*fam. sg.*) interest to work.

    _____

B. Each question is given to you in familiar form (*sg.* or *pl.*). Change each one to its corresponding polite form (*sg.* or *pl.*).

  1. ¿Te gusta la literatura?   _____

  2. ¿Os gustan los museos?   _____

  3. ¿Te interesa ir al teatro?   _____

  4. ¿Os falta el dinero?   _____

  5. ¿Te bastan 100 pesos?   _____

  6. ¿Te importa leer la revista?   _____

  7. ¿Te encanta la película?   _____

USES AND FEATURES

1. The indirect object pronoun goes immediately before a conjugated verb.

2. The indirect object pronoun may follow and be attached to an infinitive or present participle (gerund). Optionally, it may also appear immediately before the conjugated verb. We have underlined the indirect object pronoun and its corresponding prepositional phrase.

   Quiero decirle la verdad a Gloria. / *I want to tell the truth to Gloria.*
   Le quiero decir la verdad a Gloria. / *I want to tell the truth to Gloria.*

   Estoy diciéndole la verdad a Gloria. / *I'm telling the truth to Gloria.*
   Le estoy diciendo la verdad a Gloria. / *I'm telling the truth to Gloria.*

3. Remember to add a graphic accent mark when you add an indirect object pronoun to a present participle (gerund) as illustrated below.

4. **Estoy hablándole en español a él.** / *I am speaking to him in Spanish.*

5. Third person singular (**le**) and plural (**les**) indirect object pronouns must always be used. It is a "redundant" indirect object pronoun. It is not necessary in English, but it is required in Spanish. It is important to use clarifying prepositional pronouns: **a él** / *to him,* **a ella** / *to her,* **a Ud.** / *to you* (pol. sg.), **a ellos** / *to them,* **a ellas** / *to them* (all women), **a Uds.** / *to you* (pol. pl.) with these indirect object pronouns.

   Les muestro la casa a ellos. / *I show the house to them.*
   Le digo la verdad a Ud. / *I tell you the truth.*

6. The negative word **no** / *no/not* goes immediately before the direct object pronoun when that pronoun goes before the verb.

   No quiero decirle la verdad a Gloria. / *I don't want to tell the truth to Gloria.*
   No le quiero decir la verdad a Gloria. / *I don't want to tell the truth to Gloria.*

   No estoy diciéndole la verdad a Gloria. / *I'm not telling the truth to Gloria.*
   No le estoy diciendo la verdad a Gloria. / *I'm not telling the truth to Gloria.*

   No les muestro la casa a ellos. / *I'm not showing the house to them.*
   No le digo la verdad a Ud. / *I'm not telling you the truth.*

7. The verb **gustar** / *to be pleasing to* requires an indirect object pronoun. This verb is most often used in the third person singular and plural. In order to use it correctly, it is useful to rephrase sentences as follows.

   I like the book → *The book is pleasing to me.*
   In Spanish, this sentence is **Me gusta el libro**.

   I like the books → *The books are pleasing to me.*
   In Spanish, this sentence is **Me gustan los libros**.

   It is important to remember that you have to rephrase these sentences. There are other verbs that function in the same way, for example, **agradar** / *to please,* **bastar** / *to be sufficient,* **doler** (**ue**) / *to ache,* and so forth.

6

Double Object Pronoun Constructions (Indirect + Direct)

It is possible to make pronouns of both indirect and direct objects in Spanish. When there are two object pronouns, the order is always the following:

INDIRECT OBJECT PRONOUN + DIRECT OBJECT PRONOUN

In the following examples, we have used italic typeface for the indirect object pronouns. In addition, we have underlined the direct objects and their corresponding direct object pronouns. Again, remember the order for two object pronouns: indirect object pronoun + direct object pronoun.

Marina *me* **da** <u>el libro</u>. / *Marina* gives me <u>the book</u>. →

Marina *me* <u>lo</u> **da.** / *Marina gives <u>it</u> to me.*

Benito *te* **manda** <u>la carta</u>. / *Benito sends you <u>the letter</u>.* →

Benito *te* <u>la</u> **manda.** / *Benito sends <u>it</u> to you.*

Two Third Person Object Pronouns

When you use two object pronouns in a row (indirect object pronoun + direct object pronoun), and the first one of them is **le** (third person singular) or **les** (third person plural), you must change **le** or **les** to **se** as shown below. We have indicated the indirect object pronoun and its corresponding indirect object in italic typeface. We have underlined the direct object and its corresponding direct object pronoun in the examples below. You will be able to identify the indirect object pronouns in English because they are preceded by the preposition *to*.

le + direct object pronoun → **se** + direct object pronoun

les + direct object pronoun → **se** + direct object pronoun

Beatriz *le* habla <u>español</u> *a Fernando.* / *Beatriz speaks <u>Spanish</u> to Fernando.* →
Beatriz *se* <u>lo</u> habla *a él.* / *Beatriz speaks <u>it</u> (<u>Spanish</u>) to him.*

Cristóbal *les* canta <u>las canciones chilenas</u> *a Rosa y a Esteban.* / *Cristóbal sings <u>the Chilean songs</u> to Rosa and Esteban.* →
Cristóbal *se* <u>las</u> canta *a ellos.* / *Cristóbal sings <u>them</u> (<u>songs</u>) to them.*

Double Object Constructions with Infinitives and Present Participles (Gerunds)

When you use two object pronouns with an infinitive (the form of the verb that ends in **-r**), you may place them <u>before</u> the conjugated verb or <u>after</u> it, as illustrated below.

Julio quiere decir*le* <u>la verdad</u> *a Raquel.* / *Julio wants to tell <u>the truth</u> to Raquel.*→
Julio *se* <u>la</u> quiere decir *a ella.* / *Julio wants to tell <u>it</u> (<u>the truth</u>) to her.*
Julio quiere decír*se*<u>la</u> *a ella.* / *Julio wants to tell <u>it</u> (<u>the truth</u>) to her.*

When you use two object pronouns with a present participle (gerund, the form of the verb that ends in **-ndo**), you may place them <u>before</u> the conjugated verb, or <u>after</u> it, as illustrated below.

Julio está diciéndo*le* <u>la verdad</u> *a Raquel.* / *Julio is telling <u>the truth</u> to Raquel.* →
Julio *se* <u>la</u> está diciendo *a ella.* / *Julio is telling <u>it</u> (<u>the truth</u>) to her.*
Julio está diciéndo*se*<u>la</u> *a ella.* / *Julio is telling <u>it</u> (<u>the truth</u>) to her.*

Placement of Negative Word No / No, Not

When you want to make a sentence negative, you place the negative word **no** / *no, not* immediately before the double object pronouns when they precede the verb:

Julio no quiere decir*le* <u>la verdad</u> *a Raquel.* / *Julio doesn't want to tell <u>the truth</u> to Raquel.* →
Julio no *se* <u>la</u> quiere decir *a ella.* / *Julio doesn't want to tell <u>it</u> (<u>the truth</u>) to her.*
Julio no quiere decír*se*<u>la</u> *a ella.* / *Julio doesn't want to tell <u>it</u> (<u>the truth</u>) to her.*

Julio no está diciéndo*le* <u>la verdad</u> *a Raquel.* / *Julio isn't telling <u>the truth</u> to Raquel.* →
Julio no *se* <u>la</u> está diciendo *a ella.* / *Julio isn't telling <u>it</u> (<u>the truth</u>) to her.*
Julio no está diciéndo*se*<u>la</u> *a ella.* / *Julio isn't telling <u>it</u> (<u>the truth</u>) to her.*

Note

When you add two object pronouns to an infinitive (form of the verb that ends **-r**) or to a present participle or gerund (form of the verb that ends in **-ndo**), you write them as a single continuous word. We have indicated this with an <u>underline</u>. Note also the presence of a graphic accent over the last vowel in the infinitive (form of the verb ending in **-r**), which we indicate with italic typeface.

Voy a escrib*í*r<u>tela</u>. / *I'm going to write it to you.*
Estoy dici*é*ndo<u>telo</u>. / *I'm telling it to you.*

When two object pronouns come **before** a verb, they are always written as <u>separate</u> words with a space between them.

Te <u>la</u> voy a escribir. / *I'm going to write it to you.*
Te <u>lo</u> estoy diciendo. / *I'm telling it to you.*

Grammar Note

If you add **two** object pronouns (indirect and direct) to an infinitive, you must write a graphic accent mark on the place where the stress original fell to indicate that it is maintained there as illustrated below. We use italic typeface to indicate where the stress on the verb originally fell.

Voy a mostr*á*r<u>telo</u>. / *I am going to show it to you.*

If you add **one or two** pronouns to a present participle, you must write a graphic accent mark on the place where the stress originally fell to indicate that it is maintained there as illustrated below. We use italic typeface to indicate where the stress on the verb originally fell.

Estoy haci*é*ndo<u>lo</u>. / *I am doing it.*
Estoy d*á*ndo<u>telo</u>. / *I am giving it to you.*

The following chart illustrates the possible combinations with double object constructions. You may have one indirect object pronoun and one direct object pronoun (in that order) in Spanish.

Indirect Object Pronoun		Direct Object Pronoun
me		
te		lo
le → **se**		la
	+	los
nos		las
os		
les → **se**		

Exercise Set 6-1

A. Replace the indirect and direct objects with indirect and direct object pronouns. Remember that there are two options with infinitives and present participles (gerunds). In these cases, write both possibilities. Remember the order of these pronouns: indirect object pronoun + direct object pronoun.

Examples: Oscar *le* dice <u>la verdad</u> *a Dolores.*
Oscar *se* <u>la</u> dice *a ella.*

Oscar no quiere decir*le* <u>la verdad</u> *a Dolores.*
Oscar no quiere decír*se*la *a ella.*
Oscar no *se* <u>la</u> quiere decir *a ella.*

Oscar está diciéndo*le* <u>la verdad</u> *a Dolores.*
Oscar está diciéndo*se*la *a ella.*
Oscar *se* <u>la</u> está diciendo *a ella.*

1. Nicolás les escribe muchas cartas a sus padres.

_____

2. Amparo está contándole el cuento a Manolo.

_____

_____

3. Fidel necesita venderle la casa a Clara.

_____

_____

4. Ellas están dándoles el dinero a sus amigos.

_____

_____

5. Guillermo me muestra la casa.

_____

B. Provide the Spanish for the following sentences. Use an indirect object pronoun and a direct object in your answer. If there are two ways of writing the answer, please do so.

1. They sell them (*books*) to us

_____

2. We want to show them (*photos*) to them (*our friends*).

_____

_____

3. He is giving (*present participle, gerund*) it (*gift*) to her.

_____

_____

C. Answer the following questions in Spanish. Use an indirect object and a direct object pronoun in your answer.

1. ¿Le muestras las joyas a tu novia?

_____

2. ¿Vas a escribirles una carta a tus padres?

_____

_____

3. ¿Estás dándole el coche a tu hermano?

_____

_____

D. Rewrite the following affirmative sentences, and make them negative. Be sure to place the negative word in the appropriate place with respect to the object pronouns.

1. Se la (**canción**) canto a Berta.

_____

2. Se la (**verdad**) digo a mis amigos.

_____

3. Quiero hablárselo (**español**) a mi familia.

_____

4. Se lo (**juguete**) voy a regalar a mis niños.

_____

5. Estoy haciéndoselo (**café**) a mi esposa.

_____

6. Se lo (**libro**) estoy dando a ella.

_____

Exercise Set 6-2

Fill in the blanks according to the context. Use any one of the following double object combinations: **se lo**, **se la**, **se los**, **se las**. In certain contexts (following an infinitive and a present participle/gerund), the preceding words will be written as a single word with no spaces in between them.

1. Juan _____ da a ella. (**los libros**)

2. Amparo _____ está dando a mis amigos. (**el coche**)

3. Quiero mostrár_____ a Juana. (**los libros**)

4. Estoy escribiéndo _____ a mis padres. (**la carta**)

5. _____ canto a Blanca. (**la canción**)

USES AND FEATURES

Remember the following points about double object pronouns.

1. Double object pronouns appear in the following order: indirect object pronoun + direct object pronoun.

2. Double object pronouns go immediately before a conjugated verb.

3. Double object pronouns may <u>follow and be attached</u> to an <u>infinitive</u> (form of the verb ending in **-r**) or <u>present participle</u> (<u>gerund</u>, form of the verb ending in **-ndo**). When double object pronouns follow and are attached to an infinitive or present participle, they are written as a single continuous word. Optionally, they may also appear immediately <u>before</u> the conjugated verb. When the double object pronouns go before the conjugated verb, they are always written as separate words.

    Voy a mandár*te*lo. / *I am going to send <u>it</u> to you.*
    Estoy haciéndo*te*lo. / *I'm doing <u>it</u> for you.*
    Estoy diciéndo*te*lo. / *I am telling <u>it</u> to you.*

    Te <u>lo</u> **voy a mandar.** / *I am going to send <u>it</u> to you.*
    Te <u>lo</u> **estoy haciendo.** / *I'm doing <u>it</u> for you.*
    Te <u>lo</u> **estoy diciendo.** / *I am telling <u>it</u> to you.*

4. Remember that you must add a graphic accent when you add two object pronouns (indirect and direct) to an infinitive, and one or two object pronouns to a present participle (gerund) as illustrated below.

    Voy a mandár*te*lo. / *I am going to send it to you.*
    Estoy haciéndo*te*lo. / *I'm doing it for you.*
    Estoy diciéndo*te*lo. / *I am telling it to you.*

5. The third person singular (**le**) and third person plural (**les**) indirect object pronouns change to **se** when there is a following direct object pronoun. It is usually necessary to add a clarifying prepositional pronoun for these forms: **a él** / *to him*, **a ella** / *to her*, **a Ud**. / *to you* (*pol. sg.*), **a ellos** / *to them*, **a ellas** / *to them* (all women), **a Uds**. / *to you* (*pol. pl.*).

Le **muestro** <u>la casa</u> *a mi amiga.* / *I show <u>the house</u> to my girlfriend.* →
Se **la muestro** *a ella.* / *I show <u>it</u> to her.*

Voy a mostrar*le* <u>la casa</u> *a mi amiga.* / *I'm going to show <u>the house</u> to my girlfriend.* →
Voy a mostrárse*la* *a ella.* / *I'm going to show <u>it</u> to her.*

Estoy mostrándo*le* <u>la casa</u> *a mi amiga.* / *I'm showing <u>the house</u> to my girlfriend.* →
Estoy mostrándose*la* *a ella.* / *I'm showing <u>it</u> to her.*

6. The negative word **no** / *no, not* goes immediately before the double object pronouns when they are before the verb, as illustrated below.

<u>*No*</u> *se* <u>**lo**</u> **digo** *a ella.* / *I do <u>not</u> say <u>it</u> to her.*
<u>*No*</u> *se* <u>**lo**</u> **quiero decir** *a ella.* / *I do <u>not</u> want to say <u>it</u> to her.*
<u>*No*</u> *se* <u>**lo**</u> **estoy diciendo** *a ella.* / *I am <u>not</u> saying <u>it</u> to her.*

7

Reflexive Pronouns

Reflexive pronouns refer back, or reflect, the subject of a sentence. The following is a list of the reflexive pronouns in Spanish.

	Singular		Plural
1st person	**me** / *myself*	1st person	**nos** / *ourselves*
2nd person	**te** / *yourself (fam. sg.)*	2nd person	**os** / *yourselves (fam. pl.)*
3rd person	**se** / *himself, herself, yourself (pol. sg.)*	3rd person	**se** / *themselves, yourselves (pol. pl.)*

You will notice that the forms **me**, **te**, **nos**, and **os** are identical to the direct object and indirect object pronouns. The only formal difference between direct, indirect, and reflexive pronouns is in the third person singular and plural.

The following sentences exemplify typical sentences with reflexive verbs. You will note that, unlike English, the reflexive pronoun appears immediately before the conjugated verb in Spanish.

Me veo en el espejo. / *I see myself in the mirror.*

Te bañas por la mañana. / *You bathe yourself in the morning.*

Ella se divierte. / *She amuses herself.*

Nos afeitamos. / *We shave ourselves.*

Os cepilláis. / *You brush yourselves.*

Ellos se secan. / *They dry themselves.*

Conjugation of Reflexive Verbs

A verb is reflexive when it has an identical subject and direct object, as in *She dresses herself*. In English, a reflexive pronoun ends in *-self* (*sg.*) or *-selves* (*pl.*). The object is expressed as a reflexive pronoun. Reflexive verbs are thus conjugated in exactly the same manner as nonreflexive verbs, but with reflexive pronouns.

Note

A reflexive verb is identifiable by the ending **-se** (*oneself*) attached to the infinitive. Many dictionaries include the **-se** (*oneself*) as a part of verbs that are reflexive.

> **lavar<u>se</u>** / *to wash oneself*
> **ver<u>se</u>** / *to see oneself*
> **divertir<u>se</u> (ie, i)** / *to enjoy oneself*

Reflexive pronouns are placed in front of conjugated verbs.

Reflexive verbs are conjugated in exactly the same manner as other verbs with, of course, the addition of reflexive pronouns immediately before the conjugated verb.

1. Drop the reflexive ending, **-arse**; **-erse**; **-irse**.

    bañ**arse** / *to bathe oneself*
    ver**se** / *to see oneself*
    divert**irse (ie)** / *to enjoy oneself*

2. Add the regular **-ar**, **-er**, and **-ir** endings (indicated in boldface type in the tables on pages 58, 59) to the stem (indicated by an underline; see also Section 1, Chapter 1).

3. Don't forget to add the reflexive pronouns before the conjugated verb.

We provide conjugations, in the present tense, of three reflexive pronouns (**-ar**, **-er**, and **-ir** verbs):

bañarse / *to bathe oneself*

Subject Pronoun	Reflexive Pronoun	Conjugated Verb	Meaning
(yo)	**me**	bañ+**o**	*I bathe myself, I am bathing myself, I do bathe myself*
(tú)	**te**	bañ+**as**	*you (fam. sg.) bathe yourself, you are bathing yourself, you do bathe yourself*
(él, ella, Ud.)	**se**	bañ+**a**	*he, she, you (pol. sg.) bathes/bathe himself/herself/yourself, he, she, you is/are bathing himself/herself/yourself, he, she, you does/do bathe himself/herself/yourself*
(nosotros-/as)	**nos**	bañ+**amos**	*we bathe ourselves, we are bathing ourselves, we do bathe ourselves*
(vosotros/-as)	**os**	bañ+**áis**	*you (fam. pl.) bathe yourselves, you are bathing yourselves, you do bathe yourselves*
(ellos/-as, Uds.)	**se**	bañ+**an**	*they, you (pol. pl.) bathe themselves/yourselves, they, you are bathing themselves/yourselves, they, you do bathe themselves/yourselves*

The verb **verse** / *to see oneself* has an irregular first person singular form in the present tense.

verse / *to see oneself*

Subject Pronoun	Reflexive Pronoun	Conjugated Verb	Meaning
(yo)	**me**	ve+**o**	*I see myself, I am seeing myself, I do see myself*
(tú)	**te**	v+**es**	*you (fam. sg.) see yourself, you are seeing yourself, you do see yourself*
(él, ella, Ud.)	**se**	v+**e**	*he, she, you (pol. sg.) see(s) himself/herself/yourself, he, she, you is/are seeing himself/herself/yourself, he, she, you does/do see himself/herself/yourself*
(nosotros-/as)	**nos**	v+**emos**	*we see ourselves, we are seeing ourselves, we do see ourselves*
(vosotros/-as)	**os**	v+**eis**	*you (fam. pl.) see yourselves, you are seeing yourselves, you do see yourselves*
(ellos/-as, Uds.)	**se**	v+**en**	*they, you (pol. pl.) see themselves/yourselves, they, you are seeing themselves/yourselves, they, you do see themselves/yourselves*

The verb **divertirse (ie)** / *to entertain oneself* is a stem-changing verb. Remember that the endings for stem-changing verbs are regular.

divertirse (ie) / *to entertain oneself*

Subject Pronoun	Reflexive Pronoun	Conjugated Verb	Meaning
(yo)	**me**	<u>divi</u>ert+**o**	*I entertain myself, I am entertaining myself, I do entertain myself*
(tú)	**te**	<u>divi</u>ert+**es**	*you (fam. sg.) entertain yourself, you are entertaining yourself, you do entertain yourself*
(él, ella, Ud.)	**se**	<u>divi</u>ert+-	*he, she, you (pol. sg.) entertain(s) himself/herself/yourself, he, she, you is/are entertaining himself/herself/yourself, he, she, you does/do entertain himself/herself/yourself*
(nosotros-/as)	**nos**	<u>divert</u>+**imos**	*we entertain ourselves, we are entertaining ourselves, we do entertain ourselves*
(vosotros/-as)	**os**	<u>divert</u>+**ís**	*you (fam. pl.) entertain yourselves, you are entertaining yourselves, you do entertain yourselves*
(ellos/-as, Uds.)	**se**	<u>divi</u>ert+**en**	*they, you (pol. pl.) entertain themselves/yourselves, they, you are entertaining themselves/yourselves, they, you do entertain themselves/yourselves*

Common Verbs

Below are some common reflexive verbs. Note that the first set of parentheses indicates that a verb is stem-changing (e → ie; o → ue; e → i) in the present tense. The second set of parentheses indicates that the verb has a characteristic preposition, for example, **de, con, por.**

acordarse (ue) (de)	*to remember*
acostarse (ue)	*to go to bed*
afeitarse	*to shave*
bañarse	*to bathe oneself*
cansarse	*to get tired*
casarse (con)	*to get married / to marry*
cepillarse	*to brush oneself*
despertarse (ie)	*to wake up*
desvestirse (i, i)	*to get undressed*
dormirse (ue)	*to fall asleep*
ducharse	*to take a shower*
enfermarse	*to get sick*
enojarse	*.to get angry*

irse	*to go away*
lavarse	*to wash oneself*
levantarse	*to get up*
llamarse	*to call oneself / to be named*
mirarse	*to look at oneself*
peinarse	*to comb one's hair*
ponerse (la ropa)	*to put on clothing*
preocuparse (por)	*to worry (about)*
quedarse	*to remain, to stay*
quitarse	*to take off (clothing)*
secarse	*to dry oneself*
sentarse (ie)	*to sit down*
sentirse (ie, i)	*to feel (emotions, physical well-being)*
verse	*to see oneself*
vestirse (i, i)	*to dress oneself*

Note

Some verbs may have two forms: a <u>non-reflexive</u> version and a <u>reflexive</u> version. In the former case, this means that you are performing the action of the verb on someone else. In the latter version, you are performing the action on yourself. The following examples illustrate this usage. The first example in each pair is non-reflexive; the second is reflexive. You should note that when you use a verb with its non-reflexive meaning, you must use the so-called "personal **a**" with a following direct object if it refers to a person. We have indicated this with an underline in the examples below.

> **Baño <u>a</u> mi hijo.** / *I bathe my child.*
> <u>Me</u> **baño.** / *I take a bath (I bathe myself).*

> **Despierto <u>a</u> mis hijos.** / *I wake up my children.*
> <u>Me</u> **despierto.** / *I wake up.*

Many, but not all, reflexive verbs have these two meanings.

Grammar Note

In Spanish, when you refer to a part of the body or an article of clothing, you simply use the definite article. In English, however, you use the possessive adjective:

> <u>Me</u> **lavo <u>la</u> cara.** / *I wash <u>my</u> face.*
> <u>Me</u> **pongo <u>los</u> pantalones.** / *I put on <u>my</u> pants.*

The Present Progressive of Reflexive Verbs

Reflexive verbs always use reflexive pronouns in the present progressive tense, as shown below. There are, in fact, two ways of placing the reflexive pronoun. We illustrate both possibilities here. The first example shows the placement of the reflexive pronoun before the verb **estar** / *to be*. The second example shows the placement of the reflexive pronoun following and attached to the present participle (gerund). You will also note that there is a written accent over the final vowel of the present participle (gerund) ending, to indicate that the accent is retained in its original position.

Reflexive Pronoun Before Estar

lavarse / *to wash oneself*

Subject Pronoun	Reflexive Pronoun	*Estar*	Past Participle	Meaning
(yo)	**me**	<u>est</u>+**oy**	<u>lav</u>+**ando**	*I am washing myself*
(tú)	**te**	<u>est</u>+**ás**	<u>lav</u>+**ando**	*you (fam. sg.) are washing yourself yourself*
(él, ella, Ud.)	**se**	est+**á**	<u>lav</u>+**ando**	*he, she, you (pol. sg.) is/are washing himself/herself/yourself*
(nosotros-/as)	**nos**	<u>est</u>+**amos**	<u>lav</u>+**ando**	*we are washing ourselves*
(vosotros/-as)	**os**	<u>est</u>+**áis**	<u>lav</u>+**ando**	*you (fam. pl.) are washing yourselves*
(ellos/-as, Uds.)	**se**	<u>est</u>+**án**	<u>lav</u>+**ando**	*they, you (pol. pl.) are washing themselves/yourselves*

Reflexive Pronoun Follows and Attaches to Present Participle (Gerund)

lavarse / *to wash oneself*

Subject Pronoun	*Estar*	Present Participle	Meaning
(yo)	<u>est</u>+**oy**	<u>lav</u>+***ándo***+**me**	*I am washing myself*
(tú)	<u>est</u>+**ás**	<u>lav</u>+***ándo***+**te**	*you (fam. sg.) are washing yourself yourself*
(él, ella, Ud.)	<u>est</u>+**á**	<u>lav</u>+***ándo***+**se**	*he, she, you (pol. sg.) is/are washing himself/herself/ yourself*
(nosotros-/as)	<u>est</u>+**amos**	<u>lav</u>+***ándo***+**nos**	*we are washing ourselves*
(vosotros/-as)	<u>est</u>+**áis**	<u>lav</u>+***ándo***+**os**	*you (fam. pl.) are washing yourselves*
(ellos/-as, Uds.)	<u>est</u>+**án**	<u>lav</u>+***ándo***+**se**	*they, you (pol. pl.) are washing themselves/yourselves*

Reflexive Pronouns with an Infinitive

A reflexive pronoun may follow and be attached to an infinitive, or it may be placed immediately before the conjugated verb:

Quie<u>ro</u> levantar<u>me</u> tarde. / *I want to get up late.*
<u>Me</u> quie<u>ro</u> levantar tarde. / *I want to get up late.*

<u>Ella</u> <u>va</u> a vestir<u>se</u> ahora. / *She is going to get dressed now.*
<u>Ella</u> <u>se</u> <u>va</u> a vestir ahora. / *She is going to get dressed now.*

Exercise Set 7-1

A. Translate the following sentences.

1. The women wake up, get up, take a shower, and get dressed.

   _____

2. I remember today's (use **de**) date.

   _____

3. He always looks at himself in the mirror.

   _____

4. They go to bed at 11 o' clock.

   _____

5. When we work late, we get tired.

   _____

6. She worries about tests a lot.

   _____

7. If you (*fam. sg.*) don't eat well, you (*fam. sg.*) get sick.

   _____

8. He gets angry when he gets up early.

   _____

9. We fall asleep in the afternoon after lunch.

   _____

10. When they (*m.*) sit down, they (*m.*) watch TV.

    _____

11. I wash my hair.

    _____

B. Translate the following sentences. Write each sentence in two ways.

1. I am going to get married.

   _____

   _____

2. She wants to sit down.

   _____

   _____

3. They need to get up.

   _____

   _____

C. Translate the following sentences. Write each sentence in two ways. Use a present participle (gerund) in your answer.

1. We are getting tired.

   _____

   _____

2. I am getting angry.

   _____

   _____

D. Translate the following sentences.

1. I wash my son.

   _____

2. They (*m.*) wake up their children.

   _____

3. We call our parents.

   _____

4. She dresses her daughter.

   _____

5. They (*m.*) put their children to bed.

   _____

Reciprocal Reflexives

Reflexive pronouns may also be used in a construction known as the "reciprocal reflexive." Such a construction is restricted to the plural and its common English translation is "*each other*" or "*one another.*" The following examples show this usage. We have underlined and the pertinent parts of the sentences.

Nos queremos. / *We love <u>each other</u>.*

Os habláis. / <u>*You* *speak* *to one another*</u>.

Mis amigos se abrazan. / <u>*My friends embrace one another*</u>.

Los amantes se besan. / <u>*The lovers kiss each other*</u>.

Exercise Set 7-2

Translate the following sentences.

1. We embrace one another.

   _____

2. They (*m.*) know each other well.

   _____

3. You (*pol. pl.*) see one another.

   _____

4. They (*f.*) write to one another.

   _____

5. We shout at one another at times.

   _____

6. You (*m., fam. pl.*) see one another.

   _____

7. The friends buy each other gifts.

   _____

8. They (*m.*) tell each other secrets.

   _____

9. We send each other letters.

   _____

10. They (*m.*) speak to each other by telephone every day.

    _____

Reflexive Pronouns and the *Mismo* Construction

The chart below illustrates reflexive pronominal phrases after a preposition. They may be used for emphasis.

	Singular		Plural
1st person	**a mí mismo/-a** / *to myself* (*m.* and *f.*)	1st person	**a nosotros mismos** / *to ourselves* (*m.*) **a nosotras mismas** / *to ourselves* (*f.*)
2nd person	**a ti mismo/-a** / *to yourself* (*fam. sg., m.* and *f.*)	2nd person	**a vosotros mismos** / *to yourselves* (*fam. pl. m.*) **a vosotras mismas** / *to yourselves* (*fam. pl. f.*)
3rd person	**a sí mismo/-a** / *to himself, to herself to yourself* (*pol. sg., m.* and *f.*)	3rd person	**a sí mismos** / *to themselves* (*m.*) **a sí mismas** / *to themselves* (*f.*) **a sí mismos/-as** / *to yourselves* (*pol. pl., m* and *f.*)

The following examples show the use of reflexive prepositional pronominal phrases. They may be used when great emphasis is necessary. We have indicated the emphatic nature of these expressions by using CAPS in the English translation. We have underlined the subject (sometimes contained only in the verbal ending in Spanish) and the reflexive pronoun. We have also underlined the corresponding **mismo** phrase.

Me engaño a mí mismo/a. / *I deceive MYSELF.*

Te ves a ti mismo/a en el espejo. / *You see YOURSELF in the mirror.*

Ud. se habla a sí mismo/a. / *You speak to YOURSELF.*

Nos bañamos a nosotros/-as, mismos/as. / *We bathe OURSELVES.*

Os veis a vosotros/-as, mismos/as en el espejo. / *You see YOURSELVES in the mirror.*

Ellos se engañan a sí mismos/-as. / *They deceive THEMSELVES.*

In the plural form, the **mismos/-as** construction may also be used to clarify that a construction is reflexive, and not a reciprocal construction ("*one another,*" "*each other*").

Nos vemos a nosotros mismos. / *We see ourselves.*

Exercise Set 7-3

Translate the following sentences. Use the **mismo** construction according to the rules stated above.

1. You (*fam. sg., m.*) speak to yourself.

_____

2. We speak to ourselves (reflexive, not reciprocal, *m.*).

_____

3. I wash myself (*m.*).

_____

Additional Clarification of Reflexive Constructions and Reciprocal Reflexive Constructions

Sometimes, it is useful to distinguish between a reflexive construction (see the first sentence below) and a reciprocal reflexive construction (see the second sentence below).

> **<u>Nos</u> <u>vemos</u>.** / *We see ourselves.*

> **<u>Nos</u> <u>vemos</u>.** / *We see each other (one another).*

In order to make these distinctions, and to avoid ambiguity, Spanish uses certain clarifying phrases. These include such phrases as **uno/-a/-os/-as a otro/-a/-os/-as** / *each other* and **el uno al otro** / *one another.*

> **<u>Los amigos</u> <u>se</u> <u>miran</u> <u>unos a otros</u>.** / <u>*The friends look at each other*</u>.

> **<u>Los parientes</u> <u>se</u> <u>abrazan</u> <u>el uno al otro</u>.** / <u>*The relatives embrace each other*</u>.

It is also possible to use the word **mutuamente** / *mutually* to express the reciprocal meaning, as illustrated below.

> **<u>Ellos</u> <u>se</u> <u>odian</u> mutuamente.** / <u>*They hate each other*</u>.

As noted above, the use of the **mismos/-as** construction may also be used to clarify that a sentence is reflexive and not reciprocal, as seen below.

> **<u>Ellos</u> <u>se</u> <u>ven</u> <u>a sí mismos</u>.** / <u>*They see themselves*</u>.

Exercise Set 7-4

Translate the following sentences. Use a clarifying phrase as appropriate.

1. The cousins (*m.*) embrace each other.

_____

2. We see ourselves (*m.*).

_____

3. The newlyweds kiss each other frequently.

_____

4. They (*m.*) shout at one another.

_____

5. They (*m.*) look at one another.

_____

USES AND FEATURES

Remember that reflexive pronouns behave just like direct, indirect, and double object pronouns.

1. The reflexive pronoun goes immediately before a conjugated verb.

2. The reflexive pronoun may follow and be attached to an infinitive or present participle (gerund). Optionally, it may also appear immediately before the conjugated verb, as illustrated below.

   Quiero lavarme. / *I want to wash myself.*

   Me quiero lavar. / *I want to wash myself.*

   Estoy lavándome. / *I am washing myself.*

   Me estoy lavando. / *I am washing myself.*

3. Remember that you add a graphic accent mark when you add a reflexive pronoun to a present participle, as illustrated below. If the reflexive pronoun goes before the verb, no graphic accent is necessary.

   Estoy comprándome el libro. / *I am buying myself the book.*

   Me estoy comprando el libro. / *I am buying myself the book.*

4. The negative word **no** / *no/not* goes immediately before the reflexive pronoun when that pronoun goes before the verb, as illustrated below.

    No v**oy** a lavar**me**. / *I am not going to wash myself.*

    No **me** v**oy** a lavar. / *I am not going to wash myself.*

    No est**oy** comprándo**me** el libro. / *I am not buying myself the book.*

    No **me** est**oy** comprando el libro. / *I am not buying myself the book.*

5. Reciprocal constructions occur only in plural. They may be translated as "*each other*" or "*one another*" as illustrated below.

    Ellos **se** qui**eren**. / *They love one another.*

    Nos abraz**amos**. / *We embrace each other.*

6. The **mismo/-a** / *self,* **mismos/-as** / *selves* construction appears with the preposition **a** / *to, for* after a reflexive construction for emphasis or for clarification (to indicate that a construction is reflexive and **not** a reciprocal one, as illustrated below.

    Uds. **se** v**en** **a sí mismos**. / *You see yourselves.*

    Me habl**o** **a mí mismo**. / *I speak to MYSELF.*

7. The phrases **una(s) a otras(s), uno(s) a otros(s), la(s) una(s) a la(s) ostra(s), el uno al otro, los unos a los otros**, and **mutuamente** are used to clarify that a reflexive construction is in fact reciprocal, as illustrated below.

    Uds. **se** habl**an** **el uno al otro**. / *You speak to one another.*

    Uds. **se** mir**an** **unos a otros**. / *You look at each other.*

    Uds. **se** detest**an** **mutuamente**. / *You despise each other.*

8

Uses of *Se*

THE TRUE PASSIVE VOICE

The passive voice in English transposes the subject and the object of a sentence. In addition, it inserts the verb *to be* (in the same tense as the original verb) and changes the verb to its past participle form. Finally, it adds the preposition *by* before the original subject. The following diagram illustrates this process in English.

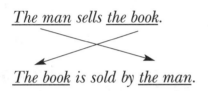

In Spanish, just as in English, sentences may appear in the passive voice. The active voice is used to indicate that the subject of the verb performs the action, whereas the passive voice is used to indicate that the subject is the receiver of the action. It is sometimes called the "true passive." As you can see in the example below, the direct object of the sentence becomes the subject of the passive voice, while the original subject becomes thc object of a prepositional phrase with **por** / *by*. Finally, the active verb **compra** / *buys* is changed to a past participle, and the corresponding form of the verb **ser** / *to be* is added with corresponding agreement with the new subject of the sentence.

Active: **Elena compra los libros.** / *Elena buys the books.*
Passive: **Los libros son comprados por Elena.** / *The books are bought by Elena.*

Here are a few additional examples of true passives.

Active	Passive
Las mujeres leen la revista. / *The women read the magazine.*	**La revista es leída por las mujeres.** / *The magazine is read by the women.*
Ellos vendieron el coche. / *They sold the car.*	**El coche fue vendido por ellos.** / *The car was sold by them.*

The *Se* Passive

While the above "true passive voice" construction is common in English, it is relatively rare in Spanish. The more common way of expressing the passive voice in Spanish, especially when you do *not* indicate "*by whom*" the action is being formed is the so-called "**se** passive" construction. In this version of the passive voice, there are two possible verb forms: third-person singular and third-person plural. These two verb forms are always preceded by the object pronoun **se**, as illustrated below. You will also note that the order of the words is as follows: **se** + verb (singular/plural) + subject (singular/plural). Note that the <u>subject</u> of the sentence appears in what is the usual <u>object</u> position in English. In this version of the passive, the subject (at the end of the sentence) refers to an object or a concept.

se	+	**verb in third-person (singular or plural)**	+	**subject (singular or plural)**

The following examples illustrate how the above formula works.

Singular	Plural
Se canta <u>la canción</u>. / *The song is sung.*	**Se cantan <u>las canciones</u>**. / *The songs are sung.*
Se habla <u>español</u> aquí. / *Spanish is spoken here.*	**Se hablan <u>español y francés</u> aquí.** / *Spanish and French are spoken here.*

It should be noted that there is another variation on this grammatical construction in which the formula is the following: **se** + verb (third person singular) + personal **a** + direct object (referring to a person):

se	+	**verb (third person singular)**	+	**Personal *a***	+	**Direct object referring to a person**

The following examples illustrate this usage.

Se eligió a Elena. / *Elena was elected.*

Se nombra a un juez hoy / *A judge is being nominated today.*

ded.

nt.

7. Friends (*m.*) are invited.

_____

8. Cars are produced in Detroit.

_____

9. Museums are closed on Mondays in Spain.

_____

10. Clothes are sold in this store.

_____

11. Popular music is played here.

_____

12. Relatives were invited.

_____

13. The president (*m.*) was elected today.

_____

14. The newspaper is published every week.

_____

Impersonal *Se*

The "impersonal **se**" construction is another common grammatical usage with **se** and the third person singular of the verb in Spanish. In this sense, there is a slightly different format from the "**se** passive" construction as illustrated below. You will also note that the order of the words is: **se** + verb (singular) + subject (singular).

se	+	verb (third-person singular)	+	subject (singular)

The following examples show how this formula works.

¿Cómo se dice *magazine* en español? / *How do you say* magazine *in Spanish?*
Se habla español en Chile. / *They speak Spanish in Chile.*
Se necesita estudiar mucho. / *One needs to study a lot.*
Se toca el piano en este edificio. / *People play the piano in this building.*

It should be noted that the English translation of the "impersonal **se**" construction may vary. The five most common English glosses for this construction in English are non-referential *you*, non-referential *they*, non-referential *we*, impersonal *one*, and generic *people*.

Exercise Set 8-2
Translate the following sentences.

1. They sell newspapers here.

   _____

2. You must eat three meals every day.

   _____

3. One should not smoke.

   _____

4. They dance the flamenco here.

   _____

5. You can't take pictures here.

   _____

6. You should exercise every day.

   _____

7. You can swim on this beach.

   _____

8. One must study every day.

_____

9. Can you enter here?

_____

10. People say that it is hot today.

USES AND FEATURES

Se constructions are very common in Spanish. In fact, they are the preferred way of expressing the passive voice in Spanish when no agent (*by* phrase) is expressed.

1. Use the formula **se** + verb (singular/plural) + subject (singular/plural) to create a **se** passive construction in Spanish, as illustrated below. Again, recall that the subject of this grammatical construction usually refers to an object or concept.

   Se hace el trabajo. / *The work is done.*
   Se estudian las lecciones. / *The lessons are studied.*

2. A variation of the above formula to express **se** + verb (third person singular) + personal **a** + direct object (referring to a person) is shown below.

   Se detiene a los sospechosos. / *The suspects are detained.*

3. Impersonal **se** constructions use the formula **se** + verb (singular) + subject (singular). The subject of the sentence is expressed by the non-referential *you, they, we,* or *one* in English:

   Se come bien en Madrid. / *You (one, they, we) eat well in Madrid.*
   Se vive bien en Santiago. / *One (you, they, we) live well in Santiago.*

9

Possessive Pronouns

A possessive pronoun indicates possession, or a relationship to, something. You will note that possessive pronouns may be masculine (*m.*) or feminine (*f.*) and singular (*sg.*) or plural (*pl.*). The reason for this is that possessive pronouns always agree in number and gender with the noun they replace.

Singular Possessive Pronouns		Plural Possessive Pronouns	
Masculine	**Feminine**	**Masculine**	**Feminine**
el mío / *mine*	**la mía** / *mine*	**los míos** / *mine*	**las mías** / *mine*
el tuyo / *yours* (*fam.*)	**la tuya** / *yours* (*fam.*)	**los tuyos** / *yours* (*fam.*)	**las tuyas** / *yours* (*fam.*)
el suyo / *his, hers, yours* (*pol.*)	**la suya** / *his, hers, yours* (*pol.*)	**los suyos** / *his, hers, yours* (*pol.*)	**las suyas** / *his, hers, yours* (*pol.*)
el nuestro / *ours*	**la nuestra** / *ours*	**los nuestros** / *ours*	**las nuestras** / *ours*
el vuestro / *yours* (*fam.*)	**la vuestra** / *yours* (*fam.*)	**los vuestros** / *yours* (*fam.*)	**las vuestras** / *yours* (*fam.*)
el suyo / *theirs, yours* (*pol.*)	**la suya** / *theirs, yours* (*pol.*)	**los suyos** / *theirs, yours* (*pol.*)	**las suyas** / *theirs, yours* (*pol.*)

You will note that a possessive pronoun is generally preceded by a definite article (*the* in English), except after the verb **ser** / *to be*, in Spanish. It is important to remember that the form of the definite article in Spanish will always agree with the noun that it refers to. This means that the definite article may be **el, la, los,** or **las**:

Singular		Plural	
Masculine	**Feminine**	**Masculine**	**Feminine**
el / *the*	**la** / *the*	**los** / *the*	**las** / *the*

The following examples illustrate this usage. Remember that the possessive pronoun always agrees in number and gender with the noun that it replaces. For this reason, it is important to review the rules for grammatical gender in Spanish.

tu lápiz / *your pencil* →
el tuyo / *yours* (agrees in number and gender with the deleted noun, *m. sg.*)

mi casa / *my house* →
la mía / *mine* (agrees in number and gender with the deleted noun, *f. sg.*)

nuestros libros / *our books* →
los nuestros / *ours* (agrees in number and gender with the deleted noun, *m. pl.*)

sus lápices / *his pencils* →
los suyos / *his* (agrees in number and gender with the deleted noun, *m. pl.*)

su pintura / *their painting* →
la suya / *theirs* (agrees in number and gender with the deleted noun, *f. sg.*)

Spanish Gender Review

Possessive pronouns agree in number (singular and plural) and in gender (masculine and feminine) with the noun they modify, or refer to. This means that you must learn the gender of nouns in Spanish. This task is relatively easy. Remember that nouns that refer to people will have the same grammatical gender as the sex of the person:

el pariente (*m.*) / *the relative*
la madre (*f.*) / *the mother*
el padre (*m.*) / *the father*
el abuelo (*m.*) / *the grandfather*
la abuela (*f.*) / *the grandmother*
el hijo (*m.*) / *the son*
la hija (*f.*) / *the daughter*
el hermano (*m.*) / *the brother*
la hermana (*f.*) / *the daughter*
el primo (*m.*) / *the cousin*
la prima (*f.*) / *the cousin*

There are two general principles for the determination of gender of Spanish nouns. First, nouns that end in **-o** are normally masculine. Those that end in **-a** are normally feminine:

Masculine:
el libro (*m.*) / the book
el cuaderno (*m.*) / *the notebook*
el teléfono (*m.*) / *the telephone*

Feminine:
la casa (*f.*) / *the house*
la computadora (*f.*) / *the computer*
la música (*f.*) / *the music*

There are a few more rules of thumb about the determination of the gender of nouns in Spanish that refer to objects or concepts.

Nouns that end in **-ma**, **-pa**, and **-ta** are normally masculine.

el tema (*m.*) / *the subject, the topic*
el mapa (*m.*) / *the map*
el planeta (*m.*) / *the planet*

Nouns that end in **-ión** are normally feminine.

la condición (*f.*) / *the condition*
la nación (*f.*) / *the nation*
la región (*f.*) / *the region*

Exceptions to the above guidelines occur, and these exceptional forms appear in frequently used nouns:

el día (*m.*) / *the day*
el avión (*m.*) / *the plane*
la mano (*f.*) / *the hand*
la foto (*f.*) / *the photo* (**foto** is an abbreviation of **fotografía**)

Plural forms include the addition of an **-s** (if the noun ends in a vowel) or an **-es** (of the noun ends in a consonant or stressed vowel) as illustrated below.

Noun ends in a vowel:

el libro (*m.*) / *the book* → **los libros** / *the books*
la casa (*f.*) / *the house* → **las casas** / *the houses*

Noun ends in a consonant or stressed vowel:

el animal (*m.*) / *the animal* → **los animales** / *the animals*
la región (*f.*) / *the region* → **las regiones** / *the regions* (no graphic accent)
el sofá (*m.*) / *the sofa* → **los sofáes** / *the sofas*

Grammar Note

Remember: Possessive pronouns agree with the item possessed and not the possessor. Possessive pronouns and pronouns always agree in gender (masculine, feminine) and number (singular, plural). If you remember this rule of thumb, you will have few problems in using the possessive pronouns.

Ambiguity in the Third Person Singular and Plural

As you may have noticed, possessive pronouns in the third person singular and plural are ambiguous:

su casa → **la suya**

La suya may mean that the house is *his, hers, yours* (*pol. sg.*), *theirs* (*m.* or *f.*), *yours* (*pol. pl.*). In conversation, the meaning of **la suya** would normally be understood by the context. In order to avoid ambiguity, however, it is possible to use the following construction:

1. Definite article (**el, la, los, las** / *the*)

2. + **de** / *of*

3. + a third person prepositional pronoun (**él** / *him*, **ella** / *her*, **Ud.** / *you*, **ellos** (*m.*) / *them*, **ellas** (*f.*) / *them*, **Uds.** / *you* (*pl.*).

By using this alternative way of expressing a possessive pronoun, the phrase above (**la suya**) may be clarified quite easily. This is useful when another person enters the conversation. The definite article agrees in gender (*m., f.*) and number (*sg., pl.*) with the deleted noun, in this case **casa** / *house*. Thus, in the expressions below, the first word **la** / *the one of* is a definite article that is feminine and singular because it agrees with, and refers to, the noun (**casa** / *house*) that has been deleted. The definite article is then followed by the preposition **de** / *of* and a prepositional pronoun: **él** / *him*, **ella** / *her*, **Ud.** (*pol. sg.*) / *you*, **ellos** (*m. pl.*) / *them*, **ellas** (*f. pl.*) / *them*, **Uds.** / *you* (*pol. pl.*).

la de él. / *his*
la de ella. / *hers*
la de Ud. / *yours* (*pol. sg.*)
la de ellos. / *theirs* (*m. pl.*)
la de ellas. / *theirs* (*f. pl.*)
la de Uds. / *yours* (*pol. pl.*)

Exercise Set 9-1

Translate the following sentences. Remember the need for agreement in number (*sg., pl.*) and gender (*m., f.*) for the possessive pronoun. When there is ambiguity, express the possessive pronoun in two ways (definite article + **de** + prepositional pronoun).

1. I have my car and she has hers.

_____

_____

2. We buy our food here and you (*fam. sg.*) buy yours here too.

_____

3. She has a black cat and mine is yellow.

_____

4. My books are at home and his are in the office.

_____

5. You (*fam. sg.*) do your task and she does hers.

_____

_____

6. My office is nearby and theirs is far away.

_____

_____

7. Our apartment is in the suburbs and yours (*pol. sg.*) is in the city.

_____

_____

8. My girlfriend is blond and his is brunette.

_____

_____

Possessive Pronouns with the Verb *Ser* / To Be

When you use a possessive pronoun after the verb **ser** / *to be*, you only use the bare pronoun. It is not necessary to use the definite article in this case:

Son mis cuadernos. / *They are my notebooks.* →
Son míos. / *They are mine* (agrees in number and gender with the deleted noun, *m. pl.*).

Es nuestra silla. / *It is our chair.* →
Es nuestra. / *It is ours* (agrees in number and gender with the deleted noun, *f. sg.*).

Son sus juguetes. / *They are her toys.* →
Son suyos. / *They are hers* (agrees in number and gender with the deleted noun, *m. pl.*).

Again, remember that you can clarify the last sentence by using a prepositional phrase. In this situation, it will be necessary to use a definite article:

Son sus juguetes. / *They are her toys.* →
Son de ella. / *They are hers.*

Exercise Set 9-2

A. Translate the following sentences. Remember the agreement in number (*sg, pl.*) and gender (*m., f.*) for the possessive pronoun. When there is ambiguity, express the possessive pronoun in two ways. Use **de** / *of* plus the prepositional pronoun.

1. The computer is mine.

   _____

2. The computers are mine.

   _____

3. The magazine is ours.

   _____

4. The magazines are ours.

   _____

5. The car is his.

   _____

6. The cars are his.

   _____

7. The dog is yours (*fam. sg.*).

   _____

8. The dogs are yours (*fam. sg.*).

   _____

9. The newspaper is theirs.

   _____

10. The newspapers are theirs.

    _____

11. The shirt is yours (*pol. sg.*).

    _____

12. The shirts are yours (*pol. sg.*).

    _____

B. Change the following sentences with possessive adjectives to sentences with possessive pronouns. When there is ambiguity, express the possessive pronoun in two ways.

1. Es mi gato.

   _____

2. Es su (*their*) mesa.

   _____

3. Son nuestras lámparas.

   _____

4. Es tu hija.

   _____

5. Es vuestro estante.

   _____

6. Es su (*their*) coche.

   _____

7. Son sus (his) zapatos.

   _____

8. Es mi café.

   _____

9. Son sus (*pol. pl.*) problemas.

   _____

10. Es nuestra playa.

   _____

Possessive Adjectives

It is important to distinguish possessive pronouns from possessive adjectives. The former are used less frequently while the latter are more common in everyday speech. Possessive adjectives allow you to express possession. They go before the noun they modify just as in English. They all agree in number (singular, plural). **Nuestro** and **vuestro** also agree in gender (masculine, feminine). Note that **tu** / *your* has no graphic accent in order to differentiate it from **tú** / *you.*

Singular Possessive Pronouns		Plural Possessive Pronouns	
Masculine	**Feminine**	**Masculine**	**Feminine**
mi / *my*	**mi** / *my*	**mis** / *my*	**mis** / *my*
tu / *your* (*fam.*)	**tu** / *your* (*fam.*)	**tus** / *your* (*fam.*)	**tus** / *your* (*fam.*)
su / *his, her, your* (*pol.*)	**su** / *his, her, your* (*pol.*)	**sus** / *his, her, your* (*pol.*)	**sus** / *his, her, your* (*pol.*)
nuestro / *our*	**nuestra** / *our*	**nuestros** / *our*	**nuestras** / *our*
vuestro / *your* (*fam.*)	**vuestra** / *your* (*fam.*)	**vuestros** / *your* (*fam.*)	**vuestras** / *your* (*fam.*)
su / *their, your* (*pol.*)	**su** / *their, your* (*pol.*)	**sus** / *their, your* (*pol.*)	**sus** / *their, your* (*pol.*)

The following are some examples of possessive adjectives. Unlike possessive pronouns, they are always used with a following noun. Remember that a possessive pronoun stands in place of a noun, so there is no noun used with a possessive pronoun.

Es <u>mi casa</u>. / *It is my house.*

Son <u>nuestros libros</u>. / *They are our books.*

Él tiene <u>su lápiz</u>. / *He has his pencil.*

You can change the above possessive adjectives to possessive pronouns by deleting the noun, as illustrated below.

Es <u>mi casa</u>. / *It is my house.* →
Es <u>la mía</u>. / *It is mine.*

Son <u>nuestros libros</u>. / *They are our books.* →
Son <u>nuestros</u>. / *They are ours.*

Él tiene <u>su lápiz</u>. / *He has his pencil.* →
Él tiene <u>el suyo</u>. / *He has his.*

Remember that the last sentence above may be expressed as follows to avoid ambiguity:

Él tiene <u>su lápiz</u>. / *He has his pencil.* →
Él tiene <u>el de él</u>. / *He has his.*

Grammar Note

There is a so-called "long form" of the possessive adjectives. These forms are identical to the possessive pronouns. However, they may appear after the noun. When they are used, their purpose is contrast or emphasis.

The "long forms" of the possessive adjectives are infrequently used. They always agree in gender (masculine, feminine) and number (singular, plural) with the noun they modify. The following examples illustrate this adjectival usage.

un libro mío / *a book of mine* (contrast)
los coches tuyos / *YOUR book* (emphasis)

USES AND FEATURES

1. Possessive pronouns agree with the noun they replace in gender (masculine, feminine) and in number (singular, plural).

2. When you use a possessive pronoun, you add the definite article that agrees in number and gender with the noun replaced, as illustrated below. Remember that the possessive pronoun <u>also</u> agrees in number and gender with the noun that it replaces.

    mis regalos / *my gifts* → **los míos** / *mine* (*m. pl.*)
    nuestro balcón / *our balcony* → **el nuestro** / *ours* (*m. sg.*)

3. After the verb **ser** / *to be*, you omit the definite article, as shown below.

    Son mis regalos. / *They are my gifts.* →
    Son míos. / *They are mine* (*m. pl.*).

    Es nuestro balcón. / It's *our balcony.* →
    Es nuestro / *It's ours* (*m. sg.*).

4. When you use the third person singular or plural of the possessive pronoun (**suyo/-a,/-os/-as**), it is sometimes necessary to use an alternative clarifying prepositional phrase with the definite article to disambiguate the sense, as illustrated below. The definite article always reflects the gender (*m., f.*) and number (*sg., pl.*) of the noun that it replaces.

    Ella tiene su libro. / *She has their book.* →
    Ella tiene el suyo. / *She has theirs.* (ambiguous)
    Ella tiene el de ellos. / *She has theirs.* (clarified)

    Es su libro. / *It's their book.* →
    Es suyo. / *It's theirs.* →
    Es de ellos. / *It's theirs.*

10

Demonstrative Pronouns

A demonstrative pronoun points out an object, concept, or person. In English, the demonstrative pronouns include *this* and *that*, *these* and *those*. Spanish makes an additional distinction by having two separate forms for *that* and *those* that correspond to relative proximity or distance from the speaker and hearer.

In order to understand the use of demonstrative **pronouns**, it is helpful to cover the demonstrative **adjectives** first, because demonstrative pronouns derive from demonstrative adjective forms.

Demonstrative Adjectives

Demonstrative adjectives, the words that express *this* / *that*, *these* / *those* generally appear <u>before</u> the noun they modify. We have indicated the agreement (number and gender) with an underline.

est<u>e</u> libr<u>o</u> / *this book*
est<u>os</u> libr<u>os</u> / *these books*
est<u>a</u> cas<u>a</u> / *this house*
est<u>as</u> cas<u>as</u> / *these houses*

There are two demonstrative adjectives for *that* and *those* in Spanish. To indicate *that* / *those* relatively near the speaker and hearer, use the forms of the demonstrative adjective **ese**.

es<u>e</u> libr<u>o</u> / *that book*
es<u>os</u> libr<u>os</u> / *those books*
es<u>a</u> cas<u>a</u> / *that house*
es<u>as</u> cas<u>as</u> / *those houses*

To indicate *that* / *those* relatively far away from the speaker and hearer (in time and space), use the forms of the demonstrative adjective **aquel** and its variants. Note that the final **l** is doubled (**l → ll**) in the feminine and plural forms (indicated in italic type).

aque*l* libr<u>o</u> / *that book*
aque*ll*<u>os</u> libr<u>os</u> / *those books*
aque*ll*<u>a</u> cas<u>a</u> / *that house*
aque*ll*<u>as</u> cas<u>as</u> / *those houses*

The following is a complete list of demonstrative adjectives in all of their forms (masculine, feminine; singular, plural).

Singular Demonstrative Adjectives		Singular Demonstrative Adjectives	
Singular	**Plural**	**Singular**	**Plural**
est_e_ / *this*	**estos** / *these*	**esta** / *this*	**estas** / *these*
es_e_ / *that (nearby)*	**esos** / *those (nearby)*	**esa** / *that (nearby)*	**esas** / *those (nearby)*
aque_l_ / *that (at a distance)*	**aque_ll_os** / *those (at a distance)*	**aque_ll_a** / *that (at a distance)*	**aque_ll_as** / *those (at a distance)*

Demonstrative Pronouns

You may change demonstrative adjectives into demonstrative pronouns by deleting the following noun. However, you must also add a graphic accent, as shown on the following table, when you make this change. Note also that the form **aquél** / *that one* has only a single **l** in the masculine form. All other forms **aquella** / *that one,* **aquéllos** / *those (ones)*, and **aquéllas** / *those (ones)* have a double **ll**.

The following table shows the forms of the demonstrative pronouns in Spanish. In addition to the masculine and feminine forms, there are also neuter forms. These are relics of earlier Latin forms and their usage will be discussed below. The masculine and feminine forms all bear a graphic accent. This is a graphic device to indicate that these forms are demonstrative pronouns and <u>not</u> demonstrative adjectives. You should note that the neuter forms do <u>not</u> have a graphic accent.

Finally, just like their demonstrative adjective counterparts, there are two forms to express *that* and *those* in Spanish. To indicate *that* and *those* relatively near the speaker and hearer, you should use **ése** / *that* and its variants. To specify that *that* and *those* are relatively far away from the speaker and hearer (in time and space), you should use **aquél** / *that* and its variants.

Masculine Demonstrative Adjectives		Feminine Demonstrative Adjectives		Neuter Demonstrative Adjectives
				One Form with No Written Accent
Singular	**Plural**	**Singular**	**Plural**	
ést_e_ / *this one*	**éstos** / *these (ones)*	**ésta** / *this one*	**éstas** / *those (ones)*	**est_o_** / *this*
és_e_ / *that one (nearby)*	**ésos** / *those (ones) (nearby)*	**ésa** / *that one (nearby)*	**ésas** / *those (ones) (nearby)*	**es_o_** / *that (nearby)*
aqué_l_ / *that one (at a distance)*	**aqué_ll_os** / *those (ones) (at a distance)*	**aqué_ll_a** / *that one (at a distance)*	**aqué_ll_as** / *those (ones)(at a distance)*	**aque_ll_o** / *that (at a distance)*

The following examples show how the transformation of a demonstrative adjective to a demonstrative pronoun works.

est<u>e</u> libr<u>o</u> / *this book* →
éste / *this one*

est<u>os</u> libr<u>os</u> / *these books* →
éstos / *these (ones)*

est<u>a</u> cas<u>a</u> / *this house* →
ésta / *this one*

est<u>as</u> cas<u>as</u> / *these houses* →
éstas / *these (ones)*

es<u>e</u> libr<u>o</u> / *that book* →
ése / *that one, nearby*

es<u>os</u> libr<u>os</u> / *those books* →
ésos / *those (ones), nearby*

es<u>a</u> cas<u>a</u> / *that house* →
ésa / *that one, nearby*

es<u>as</u> cas<u>as</u> / *those houses* →
ésas / *those (ones), nearby*

aque<u>l</u> libr<u>o</u> / *that book* →
aqué<u>l</u> / *that one, at a distance*

aque<u>llos</u> libr<u>os</u> / *those books* →
aqué<u>llos</u> / *those (ones), at a distance*

aque<u>lla</u> cas<u>a</u> / *that house* →
aqué<u>lla</u> / *that one, at a distance*

aque<u>llas</u> cas<u>as</u> / *those houses* →
aqué<u>llas</u> / *those (ones), at a distance*

Grammar Note

Note the endings of the **masculine** forms of demonstrative <u>adjectives</u>. We have used an underline to focus your attention on these endings.

est<u>e</u> / *this*
es<u>e</u> / *that (nearby)*
aque<u>l</u> / *that (at a distance)*

Note the endings of the **masculine** forms of demonstrative pronouns. Note also that they bear a written accent.

ést<u>e</u> / *this* (one)
és<u>e</u> / *that (one) (nearby)*
aqué<u>l</u> / *that (one) (at a distance)*

Finally, note the endings (**-o**) of the **neuter** forms of demonstrative pronouns.

> est**o** / *this*
> es**o** / *that (nearby)*
> aquell**o** / *that (at a distance)*

Exercise Set 10-1

Translate the following sentences.

1. This house is old but that one (nearby) is new.

   _____

2. That car (over there) is red but this one is blue.

   _____

3. These novels are interesting, but those (nearby) are terrible.

   _____

4. Those children (over there) are happy, but these are sad.

   _____

5. This book is mine, but that one (over there) is Eva's (use **de**).

   _____

6. I like that color (nearby), but not this one.

   _____

7. I have this movie, but not that one (over there).

   _____

8. These neighbors (nearby) are nice, but those (nearby) are unpleasant.

   _____

Neuter Demonstrative Pronouns

The so-called neuter demonstrative pronouns are used when you want to refer to something generic or nonspecific, such as unspecified notions, concepts, ideas, or situations in a general or hypothetical sense. The following are some typical examples. Remember that these forms do not have a graphic accent.

> **¡Esto es ridículo!** / *This is ridiculous!*
> **Eso es un problema.** / *That is a problem.*
> **Aquello está lejos.** / *That (unspecified thing in the distance) is far away.*

Exercise Set 10-2

Translate the following sentences.

1. That is stupid!

_____

2. This is my error.

_____

3. That (over there) is a problem.

_____

The Former and the Latter

The English notion of *the former* and *the latter* may be expressed in Spanish by the use of the demonstrative pronouns **éste ... aquél**. It should be noted that **éste** refers to the more recent or closer noun, while **aquél** refers to the more remote noun. Thus, the Spanish usage is the reverse of the English, as illustrated in the following example.

> **Benito** y *Claudia* **son hermanos. *Ésta* es alta y <u>aquél</u> es bajo.** / *Benito and Claudia are brother and sister. <u>The latter</u> is short and <u>the former</u> is tall.*

Exercise Set 10-3

Translate the following sentence.

1. I have two daughters and two sons. The former are brunette and the latter are blond.

_____

USES AND FEATURES

1. Demonstrative pronouns agree in gender (masculine, feminine) and number (singular, plural) with the noun they replace.

2. Demonstrative pronouns bear a graphic accent (except for the neuter forms **esto** / *this*, **eso** / *that*, **aquello** / *that*).

11

Adjectives as Pronouns

There are two types of adjectives in both Spanish and English. The first is called a descriptive adjective, and, as its name implies, it describes some aspect of the noun to which it refers, for example, color, shape, size, nationality, and so forth. In Spanish, these adjectives normally appear <u>after</u> the noun they modify.

The second type of adjective, called a limiting adjective, normally appears <u>before</u> the noun it modifies, it includes definite (*the*), and indefinite articles (*a, an*), possessive adjectives (*my, your*, and so forth), demonstrative adjectives (*this* and *that; these* and *those*), quantifiers (*many, few, some*, and so forth), cardinal numbers (*one, two, three*, and so forth), and ordinal numbers (*first, second, third*, and so forth).

Tip
You can remember the word order in Spanish of limiting and descriptive adjectives with the following mnemonic aid: LAND. It means **L**imiting **A**djectives precede the **N**oun while **D**escriptive adjectives follow it. This memory aid really helps to recall this word order difference between Spanish and English.

Descriptive Adjective Pronouns

Adjectives may be used as pronouns, that is, they stand in the place of nouns, by deleting the noun to which the adjective refers. Recall also that descriptive adjectives normally follow the noun to which they refer. In English, there is often a "trace" of the deleted noun, that is, the word *one* or *ones* is added to indicate that a noun was eliminated. In the following examples, the first set contains the definite article (*the*) while the second set contains indefinite articles (*a, an*).

el <u>hombre</u> cansado / *the tired man* → **el cansado** / *the tired one*
la <u>mujer</u> alta / *the tall woman* → **la alta** / *the tall one*
los <u>hombres</u> cansados / *the tired men* → **los cansados** / *the tired ones*
las <u>mujeres</u> altas / *the tall women* → **las altas** / *the tall ones*

un <u>hombre</u> alto[*] / *a tall man* → **un alto** / *a tall one*
una <u>mujer</u> rubia / *a blond woman* → **una rubia** / *a blond one*

---

[*] Note: when the word **uno** represents a previously expressed noun, there is no apocopation to **un** (**un coche rojo** / *a red car* → **uno rojo** / *a red one*). However, an adjective that represents and refers to a person requires the apocopated form **un** (**un hombre alto** / *a tall man* → **un alto** / *a tall one*).

The process of converting an adjective to a pronoun simply involves the deletion of the noun, which we illustrate here by means of an underlined gap. You will note that you must retain gender (*m.*, *f.*) and number (*sg.*, *pl.*) agreement with the omitted noun.

el <u>coche</u> rojo / *the red car*→ **el _____ rojo** (**el rojo**) / *the red one*
los <u>lápices</u> amarillos / *the yellow pencils* → **los _____ <u>amarillos</u>** (**los amarillos**) / *the yellow ones*

Exercise Set 11-1

A. Rewrite the following noun phrases, and change the noun phrases into adjective pronouns.

1. los bolígrafos azules

   _____

2. la casa grande

   _____

3. las canciones populares

   _____

4. la comida mexicana

   _____

5. el coche viejo

   _____

6. las hermanas bonitas

   _____

7. el libro interesante

   _____

8. los amigos mexicanos

   _____

9. la torta sabrosa

   _____

10. los animales domésticos

   _____

11. el globo rojo

   _____

B. Translate the following sentences.

1. I eat big meals and she eats small ones.

_____

2. The black car is mine, and the gray one is yours (*fam. sg.*).

_____

3. The blond woman is my sister and the redheaded one is my cousin.

_____

4. I have a blue car and my wife has a yellow one.

_____

5. I have old toys, but the new ones are my son's (use **de**).

_____

The Neuter Definite Article

There is a neuter definite article **lo** / *the*. The neuter article **lo** used with a following adjective creates a pronoun that refers to the properties of the adjective in the abstract. The English translation is sometimes rendered as *that which is, what is, the part*, or simply, *the* + adjective. When you use **lo** with a possessive adjective, you must use the "long forms" (see Chapter 9).

   lo bueno y lo malo / *good and evil* (*that which is good, that which is evil*)
   lo moderno / *that which is modern*
   lo hecho / *what is done*
   lo curioso / *the curious part*
   lo antiguo / *the ancient*
   lo tuyo / *what is yours*
   lo mío / *that which is mine*

Exercise Set 11-2

Translate the following sentences.

1. The old and the new

_____

2. What is useful

_____

3. What is mine

_____

4. That which is current

_____

5. The past

_____

Limiting Adjectives

Limiting adjectives normally go before a noun. This type of adjectives quantifiers (*many, few, some,* and so forth), ordinal numbers (*first, second, third,* and so forth), possessive adjectives, and demonstrative adjectives. We have already studied the uses of possessive adjectives and their related pronominal forms (see Chapter 9) and of demonstrative adjectives and their related pronominal forms (see Chapter 10), so we will not repeat that material here.

Ordinal Numbers

Ordinal numbers are adjectives and they agree in number (*sg., pl.*) and gender (*m. f.*) with the noun to which they refer. The following are a few examples. Note that the final **-o** of **primero** / *first* and **tercero** / *third* is deleted before a following masculine singular noun. We have underlined the ordinal numbers in Spanish and English.

> **el <u>primer</u> hombre** / *the <u>first</u> man*
> **la <u>segunda</u> mujer** / *the <u>second</u> woman*
> **el <u>tercer</u> lápiz** / *the <u>third</u> pencil*
> **la <u>cuarta</u> silla** / *the <u>fourth</u> chair*

You can change the ordinal numbers (ordinal numerical adjectives) above to pronouns by deleting the following noun. Ordinal numbers agree in number (*sg., pl.*) and gender (*m., f.*) with the noun they modify. Note that when you delete a following masculine noun in Spanish, you retain the following **-o** of the two ordinal numbers **primer<u>o</u>** / *first* and **tercer<u>o</u>** / *third*. We repeat the above examples to illustrate this procedure.

> **el <u>primer</u> hombre** / *the <u>first</u> man* → **el <u>primero</u>** / *the <u>first one</u>*
> **la <u>segunda</u> mujer** / *the <u>second</u> woman* → **la <u>segunda</u>** / *the <u>second one</u>*
> **el <u>tercer</u> lápiz** / *the <u>third</u> pencil* → **el <u>tercero</u>** / *the <u>third one</u>*
> **la <u>cuarta</u> silla** / *the <u>fourth</u> chair* → **la <u>cuarta</u>** / *the <u>fourth one</u>*

Common Ordinal Numbers

primer(o)	*first*	**sexto**	*sixth*
segundo	*second*	**séptimo**	*seventh*
tercer(o)	*third*	**octavo**	*eighth*
cuarto	*fourth*	**noveno**	*ninth*
quinto	*fifth*	**décimo**	*tenth*

Exercise Set 11-3

Translate the following sentences.

1. The first test is harder than the second one.

   _____

2. My house is the fourth on the right and my friends live in the fifth.

   _____

3. The first month is January. The seventh is July, and the ninth is September.

   _____

4. The second novel is better than the first one.

   _____

5. The eighth symphony is better than the fourth.

   _____

Cardinal Numbers

Cardinal numbers go immediately before a noun. They are sometimes called *quantifiers* because they indicate the quantity of an item before a noun. They may function as a pronoun when the following noun is deleted. The following examples illustrate how this process works. We have underlined the cardinal numbers used as a pronoun.

Tengo un coche. / *I have one car.* → **Tengo <u>uno</u>.** / *I have <u>one</u>.*
Prefiero dos frutas. / *I prefer two fruits.* → **Prefiero <u>dos</u>.** / *I prefer <u>two</u>.*
Compro diez libros. / *I'm buying ten books.* → **Compro <u>diez</u>.** / *I'm buying <u>ten</u>.*
Tengo doscientas revistas. / *I have two hundred magazines.* → **Tengo <u>doscientas</u>.** / *I have <u>two hundred</u>.*

Note

The cardinal number *one* does not have a final **-o** before a following masculine noun, as shown below.

Quiero <u>un</u> libro. / *I want <u>one</u> book.*
Quiero <u>uno</u>. / *I want <u>one</u>.*

The cardinal number *one* agrees in gender (*f.*) with a following feminine noun, as shown below.

Quiero <u>una</u> revista. / *I want <u>one</u> magazine.*
Quiero <u>una</u>. / I want <u>one</u>.

It should also be noted that in the above sentences **un** and **una** may also be interpreted as a definite article *a*. The context will indicate the appropriate meaning.

Furthermore, you delete the final **-o** before a following masculine noun with cardinal numbers such as *21, 31, 41,* and so forth:

Tengo veintiún libros. / *I have twenty-one books.* →
Tengo <u>veintiuno</u>. / *I have <u>twenty-one</u>.*

Tengo treinta y un libros. / *I have thirty-one books.* →
Tengo <u>treinta y uno</u> / *I have <u>thirty-one</u>.*

Tengo cuarenta y un libros. / *I have forty-one books.* →
Tengo <u>cuarenta y uno</u>. / *I have <u>forty-one</u>.*

Finally, the numbers *200* to *900* agree in gender (*m., f.*) with the noun they modify:

Leí trescientas páginas. / *I read three hundred pages.* →
Leí <u>trescientas</u>. / *I read <u>three hundred</u>.*

Encontré quinientos libros. / *I found five hundred books.* →
Encontré <u>quinientos</u>. / *I found <u>five hundred</u>.*

Common Cardinal Numbers

1	un(o)	17	diecisiete	50	cincuenta		
2	dos	18	dieciocho	60	seisenta		
3	tres	19	diecinueve	70	setenta		
4	cuatro	20	veinte	80	ochenta		
5	cinco	21	veintiun(o)	90	noventa		
6	seis	22	veintidós	100	cien, ciento		
7	siete	23	veintitrés	200	doscientos		
8	ocho	24	veinticuatro	300	trescientos		
9	nueve	25	veinticinco	400	cuatrocientos		
10	diez	26	veintiséis	500	quinientos		
11	once	27	veintisiete	600	seiscientos		
12	doce	28	veintiocho	700	setecientos		
13	trece	29	veintinueve	800	ochocientos		
14	catorce	30	treinta	900	novecientos		
15	quince	31	treinta y un(o)	1.000	mil		
16	dieciséis	40	cuarenta				

Exercise Set 11-4

Translate the following sentences.

1. My friend has few books, but I have three hundred.

_____

2. Enrique has two cars, and I have one.

_____

3. I have one computer, but I need two.

_____

4. Elena's (use **de**) family has four cellular telephones, but we have only one.

_____

5. I have one cat, but Carmen has three.

_____

Quantifiers as Adjective Pronouns

There are limiting adjectives that are sometimes called *quantifiers* (same as cardinal numbers) because they indicate *how much* or *how many* are involved. It is possible to omit the following noun so that the quantifiers stand in the place of the noun that is omitted:

Muchas mujeres trabajan aquí. / *Many women work here.* → **Muchas trabajan aquí.** / *Many work here.*

Tengo poco dinero. / *I have little money.* → **Tengo <u>poco</u>.** / *I have <u>little</u>.*

¿Tiene Ud. otro libro? / *Do you have another book?* → **¿Tiene Ud. <u>otro</u>?** / *Do you have <u>another one</u>?*

Leo varias novelas. / *I'm reading several novels.* → **Leo <u>varias</u>.** / *I'm reading <u>several</u>.*

Common Quantifiers

algun(o)/-a*	*some*	**otros/-as**	*others*
algunos/-as	*some*	**poco/-a**	*little*
ambos/-as	*both*	**pocos/-as**	*few*
demasiado/-a	*too much*	**todo/-a**	*every*
demasiados/-as	*too many*	**todos/-as**	*all*
mucho/-a	*much, a lot*	**uno/-a**	*a, one*
muchos/-as	*many*	**unos/-as**	*some, a few*
ningun(o)*	*no, none*	**varios/-as**	*various, several*
otro/-a	*other, another*		

Exercise Set 11-5

Translate the following sentences. The nouns in parentheses indicate the gender and number to be used in the pronouns.

1. I have too much (*work*).

   _____

2. She needs one (*notebook*).

   _____

3. Few (*stores*) are open now.

   _____

4. María drinks a lot (*milk*).

   _____

---

* Alguno and ninguno become shortened to **algún** and **ningún** before a following masculine singular noun as shown below. When they are shortened, they bear a graphic accent.

    algún libro / *some book*

    ningún hombre / *no man*

5. They (*m.*) offer several (*discounts*).

_____

6. We sell both (*versions*).

_____

7. I have some (*photos*) here.

_____

8. He wants several (*suggestions*).

_____

9. We have another one (*idea*)

_____

10. Others (*students*) are going to the library.

_____

Indefinite and Negative Pronouns

The following are two common indefinite pronouns and their corresponding negative pronoun counterparts. **Algo** / *something* and **nada** / *nothing* refer to things or to objects, while **alguien** / *someone* and **nadie** / *no one* refer to people.

Indefinite Word	**Negative Word**
algo / *something*	**nada** / *nothing*
alguien / *someone*	**nadie** / *no one*

Grammar Note

It should be noted that when you place a negative word after the verb, you must place the word **no** before the verb, as shown below. You will recall that in conventional English grammar double negatives are not acceptable.

No hay nada. / *There is nothing.*

No veo a nadie. / *I see no one.* / *I don't see anyone.*

The following two indefinite and negative forms are adjectives. They function as pronouns when the following noun is omitted.

algun(o)/-a/-os/-as / *some*   **ningun(o)/-a** / *no* (no plural form)

The above forms may be used as pronouns:

¿Tienes algunas novelas? / *Do you have some novels?* → **¿Tienes <u>algunas</u>?** / *Do you have <u>some</u>?*

No tengo ninguna novela. / *I don't have a novel.* → **No tengo <u>ninguna</u>.** / *I have <u>none</u>.*

Grammar Note
Note that **ningun(o)/-a** / *no, none* normally appears in the singular even if the referent is plural.

Grammar Note
It is necessary to use the personal **a** before **alguien** / *someone* and **nadie** / *no one*. Likewise, when **algun(o)/-a** / *some* and **ningun(o)/-a** / *no, none* refer to a person, a personal **a** is necessary (see Section II, Chapter 1 for further discussion). The following examples with the personal **a** underlined illustrate this point. **No veo <u>a</u> nadie.** / *I see no one.* **¿Ves <u>a</u> alguien?** / *Do you see someone?* **No recuerdo <u>a</u> ninguno.** / *I remember no one.* **Reconozco <u>a</u> algunos.** / *I recognize some.*

Exercise Set 11-6

Translate the following sentences.

1. Is someone coming?

_____

2. No one is coming.

_____

3. Do you (*fam. sg.*) have something?

_____

4. I have nothing.

_____

5. Do you (*fam. sg.*) need some recipes?

_____

6. I have none (*recipes*).

_____

USES AND FEATURES

1. There are two basic types of adjectives: limiting and descriptive. Limiting adjectives normally precede nouns, while the descriptive adjectives normally follow nouns. Limiting adjectives include categories of words such as definite articles (*the*), indefinite articles (*a, an*), possessive adjectives, demonstrative adjectives, quantifiers (*many, few, some,* and so forth), cardinal numbers (*one, two, three,* and so forth), and ordinal numbers (*first, second, third,* and so forth). Descriptive adjectives describe the noun to which they refer (size, color, shape, nationality, and so forth), and they normally appear after the noun they modify.

2. To make an adjective a pronoun, you simply omit the noun. The context will allow speaker and hearer to understand what the reference is, as illustrated below.

    Compré el coche azul ayer y Alba compró <u>el rojo</u> anteayer. / *I bought the blue car yesterday and Alba bought <u>the red one</u> the day before yesterday.*

3. Adjectives always agree in number (*sg., pl.*) with the noun they modify. They frequently agree in gender (*m., f.*) with the noun they modify. When you use an adjective as a pronoun, you maintain gender and number agreement with the noun omitted, as illustrated below. We leave an underline in the Spanish example to indicate where the noun has been omitted.

    la primera cita / *the first date* → **la primera** _____ / *the <u>first one</u>*
    ciertos libros / *certain books* → **ciertos** _____ / *<u>certain ones</u>*
    trescientos sesenta y cinco días / *three hundred sixty-five days* → **trescientos sesenta y cinco** _____ / *<u>three hundred sixty-five</u>*

4. The neuter definite article **lo** / *the* may be used with adjectives to refer to the meaning of the adjective in an abstract way, as illustrated below.

    lo cierto / *the certain part*
    lo imposible / *that which is impossible*

5. A few indefinite and negative pronouns exist. When they appear after the verb, you must place the negative word **no** / *no, not* before the verb, as illustrated below. Remember that in standard English, there is only one negative per sentence.

    <u>No</u> hay <u>nadie</u> aquí / *There is <u>no one</u> here.*
    <u>No</u> tengo <u>ninguno</u>. / *I have <u>none</u>.*

12

Relative Pronouns

RELATIVE CLAUSES

A relative clause is a sentence contained within another sentence. In simple terms, a *clause* is a group of related words that contains a subject and a verb, and it is a subordinated part of the main sentence. Relative pronouns are used in relative clauses. A relative pronoun refers to an *antecedent,* which is a noun that appears before the relative pronoun. It should be noted that relative clauses are sometimes called *adjectival clauses* because the entire clause functions as an adjective that describes some aspect of the antecedent noun to which it refers.

The following sentence in English is an example of a relative clause. The noun phrase *the man* is known as an antecedent. It is the word to which the relative clause refers. The word *who* is a relative pronoun, and it introduces the relative clause. We have underlined the antecedent and the relative pronoun, as well as the entire relative clause to help you to visualize this process and format.

I visit the man who is sick.

In the above sentence, the word *who* refers to the noun phrase *the man.* This type of grammatical construction allows you to avoid the repetition of the noun phrase *the man* in two separate sentences, as shown below. It also makes it possible to combine two sentences into one single sentence. This process, technically known as "*relativization,*" occurs in all languages.

I visit the man. The man is sick.

Likewise, in the following sentence the relative pronoun *that* refers to the antecedent *the book.* We have underlined the antecedent and the relative pronoun, as well as the entire relative clause to help you to visualize this process and format.

I read the book that is interesting.

Once again, the above sentence is a combination of two simple sentences, as shown below.

I read <u>the book</u>. <u>The book</u> is interesting.

RELATIVE PRONOUNS IN SPANISH

The following table contains a list of the relative pronouns to be discussed in this chapter in the order of their appearance. Remember that the clause to the right of the relative pronoun is always the relative clause.

Spanish Relative Pronoun	English Relative Pronoun
que	*who, that, which*
(a) quien (*sg.*)	*who(m)* (*sg.*)
(a) quienes (*pl.*)	*who(m)* (*pl.*)
el cual (*m. sg.*) **la cual** (*f. sg.*)	*who, which* (*sg.*)
los cuales (*m. pl.*) **las cuales** (*f. pl.*)	*who, which* (*pl.*)
el que (*m. sg.*) **la que** (*f. sg.*)	*who, which* (*sg.*)
los que (*m. pl.*) **las que** (*f. pl.*)	*who, which* (*pl.*)
cuyo (*m. sg.*) **cuya** (*f. sg.*)	*whose*
cuyos (*m. pl.*) **cuyas** (*f. pl.*)	*whose*
lo que (*neuter*) **lo cual** (*neuter*)	*that which, what, which*

Restrictive and Nonrestrictive Relative Clauses

In order to understand what a relative pronoun is, it is helpful to talk about two types of clauses in which a relative pronoun may appear. The first is called a *restrictive* relative clause. This is a clause that gives essential meaning to a sentence by providing some uniquely identifying characteristic of the antecedent.

The following sentence shows a restrictive relative clause. Its use is essential to the meaning of the sentence because it provides uniquely identifying information about the antecedent (*a book*).

> **Un libro que no tiene páginas es inútil**. / *A book that has no pages is useless.*

If you remove the relative clause, the meaning would be very different, as illustrated below.

> **Un libro […] es inútil**. / *A book […] is useless.*

The second type of relative clause, a *nonrestrictive* clause, is that which normally appears in printed form between commas. In speech, it is marked by a pause. The following sentence shows this type of relative clause.

> **Estos libros, que tienen cuentos interesantes y aventureros, son fascinantes**. / *These books, which have interesting and adventurous stories, are fascinating.*

This sentence may have the nonrestrictive clause deleted with no major meaning loss, as illustrated below.

> **Estos libros […] son fascinantes**. / *These books […] are fascinating.*

Grammatical Functions of Relative Pronouns

The following sentences illustrate that relative pronouns may be, respectively, subject, direct object, indirect object, or object of a preposition in a relative clause. We have underlined the antecedent and the relative pronoun. We have also underlined the entire relative clause to help you to visualize this process.

1. Subject in a relative clause.

    > **Vemos a la profesora que enseña español**. / *We see the professor who teaches Spanish.*

2. Direct object in a relative clause.

    > **Éste es el libro que compré ayer**. / *This is the book that I bought yesterday.*

3. Indirect object in a relative clause.

    > **Éste es el hombre a quien le di el dinero**. / *This is the man to whom I gave the money.*

4. Object of a preposition in a relative clause.

    > **La persona de quien dependo es mi esposa**. / *The person on whom I depend is my wife.*

The Relative Pronoun Que

The most useful, and the most frequent, relative pronoun in Spanish is **que** / *who, that, which*. It is invariable in form (both gender and number), but its uses, as illustrated below, are varied.

Again, recall that the relative pronoun **que** may be a subject, direct object, or object of a preposition of a relative clause. We have underlined the antecedent and the relative pronoun. We have also underlined the entire relative clause.

1. Subject.

   El hombre que trabaja mucho gana mucho. / *The man who works a lot earns a lot.*

2. Direct object.

   La revista que compré ayer es cara. / *The magazine that I bought yesterday is expensive.*

3. Object of a preposition.

   La ciudad en que vivo tiene muchos cafés. / *The city in which I live has many cafes.*

Tip
Remember that in English it is possible to eliminate the relative pronoun, but in Spanish this is **never** permitted. We use parentheses to indicate this option in English. **Los libros que necesito están aquí.** / *The books (that) I need are here.* **Veo a la mujer que conoces.** / *I see the woman (who[m]) you know.* **Tengo los apuntes que buscas.** / *I have the notes (that) you are looking for.*

Grammar Note
To refer to an antecedent that is an object or a concept, you normally use **que** after the following common prepositions: **a** / *to, at,* **con** / *with,* **de** / *of, from,* **en** / *in, on.* **Los apuntes a que me refiero son éstos.** / *The notes to which I refer are these.* **El bolígrafo con que escribo es mi favorito.** / *The pen with which I write is my favorite.* **El coche de que dependo está allí.** / *The car on which I depend is there.* **Las notas en que te interesas son buenas.** / *The grades in which you are interested are good.*

Note

In Spanish, when you use a preposition with a relative pronoun, the preposition **always** precedes the relative pronoun. In English, it is possible to "*strand,*" or place the preposition at the end of the clause or sentence. You can never "*strand,*" or put a preposition at the end of sentence in Spanish.

> **El cuento de que hablé es de Horacio Quiroga.** / *The short story that I spoke about is by Horacio Quiroga.*

In English, it is possible to use the Spanish word order, but it sounds formal or stilted, as illustrated below.

> **El cuento de que hablé es de Horacio Quiroga.** / *The short story about which I spoke is by Horacio Quiroga.*

In English, it is also possible to omit the relative pronoun in the previous two sentences. This is **never** possible in Spanish.

> **El cuento de que hablé es de Horacio Quiroga.** / *The short story I spoke about is by Horacio Quiroga.*

Grammar Note

It is important to note that there is another grammatical form **que** / *that* which is <u>not</u> a relative pronoun. This **que**, called a conjunction, is used to introduce noun clauses. This conjunction (**que** / *that*) has <u>no antecedent</u>.

> **Creo que llueve mucho.** / *I think that it is raining hard.* (no antecedent)

You can tell the difference between the <u>relative pronoun</u> **que** and the <u>conjunction</u> **que** because the relative pronoun always refers to an immediately preceding antecedent, while the conjunction has a verb immediately preceding. Compare the following sentences.

> **El dinero que necesito está aquí.** / *The money that I need is here.* (antecedent)

> **Espero que no llueva.** / *I hope that it is not raining.* (no antecedent)

Exercise Set 12-1

Translate the following sentences.

1. She has the tickets that I want.

   _____

2. I see the man who is going to the store.

   _____

3. The gift, which is expensive, is in the car.

   _____

4. This is the woman who wants to go to the office.

   _____

5. There are many students who want to go to the library.

   _____

6. I have the report that you are looking for.

   _____

7. The woman who is in the office is my cousin.

   _____

8. The computer that I like is here.

   _____

9. I walk through the park that is in the downtown area.

   _____

10. I see the woman who teaches my class.

    _____

The Relative Pronouns *Quien* and *Quienes*

Quien / *who* and **quienes** / *who* are <u>only</u> used to refer to people. These relative pronouns agree in number (singular or plural) with the antecedent. We have underlined the antecedent and the relative pronoun. We have also underlined the entire relative clause to help you to visualize this process.

You use **quien** or **quienes** in *nonrestrictive* relative clauses, that is, those marked off in print by commas. You may also use **que** / *who* in nonrestrictive relative clauses:

> **<u>Esa mujer</u>, <u>quien (que) es muy es muy inteligente</u>, es mi estudiante.** / *<u>That woman</u>, <u>who is very intelligent</u>, is my student.*

> **<u>Esos hombres</u>, <u>quienes (que) están cansados</u>, acaban de llegar.** / *<u>Those men</u>, <u>who are tired</u>, have just arrived.*

When referring to people in restrictive relative clauses, after simple prepositions (**a** / *to, at;* **con** / *with;* **de** / *of, from;* **en** / *on*), you will use **quien** / *whom* or **quienes** / *whom* as illustrated below. In informal, or colloquial English, the preposition often appears at the end of the sentence.

> **Elena es <u>la mujer</u> <u>a quien le mando la tarjeta</u>.** / *Elena is <u>the woman to whom I send the card</u>. (Elena is <u>the woman who I send the card to.</u>)*

> **Mi compañero de clase <u>con quien estudio</u> es muy inteligente.** / *<u>My classmate with whom I study</u> is very intelligent.*

> **El señor Rodríguez es <u>la persona de quien recibí el regalo</u>.** / *Mr. Rodríguez is <u>the person from whom I received the gift</u>. (Mr. Rodríguez is <u>the person I received the gift from.</u>)*

> **Éstas son <u>las personas</u> <u>en quienes pienso</u>.** / *These are <u>the people about whom I think</u>. (These are <u>the people who I think about.</u>)*

You may also use the personal **a** (see Section Two, Chapter 1, Grammar Note for more details) with **quien** or **quienes** / *whom* in a nonrestrictive relative clause as illustrated below. In this case **a quien** / *whom* is the direct object of the verb (**ves** / *you see*) in the nonrestrictive relative clause and not the subject.

> **<u>María</u>, <u>a quien ves</u>, habla por teléfono.** / *<u>Mary</u>, <u>who(m) you see</u>, is talking on the phone.*

Exercise Set 12-2

Translate the following sentences.

1. Berta, who is from Guatemala, is here.

   _____

2. My relatives, who live in Chicago, speak many languages.

   _____

3. Alicia, beside whom you (*fam. sg.*) are seated, is famous.

   _____

4. Juan, whom you (*fam. sg.*) know, is a student at the university.

   _____

5. My girlfriend, who is from Madrid, lives here now.

   _____

6. The friends whom we invited are late.

   _____

7. The woman with whom you (*fam. sg.*) are dancing is Graciela.

   _____

8. Federico is the person for whom she makes many sacrifices.

_____

9. The girl, who eats a lot of ice cream, has a brother.

_____

10. The doctor whom we know is very good.

_____

The Relative Pronouns *El Cual* and *El Que*

The relative pronouns **el cual** / *which, who, whom* and **el que** / *which, who, whom* may have antecedents that refer to persons, objects, or concepts. The **el** part of the relative pronoun **el cual** changes for gender and number (**el cual, la cual, los cuales, las cuales**) and the **cual** part of **el cual** changes for number (**cual, cuales**). **El cual** may be used after simple and compound prepositions.

The **el** part of the relative pronoun **el que** / *which, who, whom* changes for gender and number (**el que, la que, los que, las que**). The **que** part of the relative pronoun **el que**, however, is invariable (**que**). The following chart shows all of the possible manifestations of these relative pronouns.

Masculine		Feminine	
Singular	**Plural**	**Singular**	**Plural**
el cual	los cuales	la cual	las cuales
el que	los que	la que	las que

It is best to go through this section of the chapter step-by-step to understand the use of these relative pronouns. The following sets of examples allow you to see how these relative pronouns are used. We have underlined the antecedent and the relative pronoun, as well as the entire relative clause.

1. Use of **el cual** and **el que** and their various manifestations in <u>nonrestrictive</u> relative clauses. Note that is also possible to use **quien** / *who* or **quienes** / *who* in nonrestrictive relative clauses when you refer to people.

   <u>Mis amigos, los cuales (los que) (quienes) estudian mucho,</u> son interesantes. / <u>*My friends, who study a lot,*</u> *are interesting.*

   <u>La química, la cual (la que) es difícil,</u> es fácil para mí. / <u>*Chemistry, which is difficult,*</u> *is easy for me.*

2. Use of **el cual** in place of **quien(es)** and **que**.

    El cual, although more formal and less common, may be used in place of **quien(es)** and **que** in <u>nonrestrictive</u> relative clauses. Thus, the first sentence in # 1 above may also have the following alternative relative pronouns.

    <u>**Mis amigos**, **los cuales (quienes, que) estudian mucho**, **son interesantes.**</u> / <u>My friends</u>, <u>who study a lot</u>, are interesting.

3. Use of **el cual** to avoid ambiguity.

    El cual is used to avoid ambiguity when there are two preceding nouns, either one of which may be a possible antecedent to the relative pronoun, especially when it is of different gender or number, as seen in the following examples. We have underlined the antecedent, the relative pronoun, and the entire relative clause:

    <u>**El color** de mi casa, **el cual me gusta mucho**, es blanco.</u> / <u>The color</u> of my house, <u>which I like a lot</u>, is white.

    <u>**Las amigas** de Ramón, **las cuales son muy inteligentes**, son simpáticas.</u> / <u>The girlfriends</u> of Ramón, <u>who are very intelligent</u>, are nice.

4. Use of **el que** to refer to an understood antecedent.

    El que / *the one who* is used to refer to an <u>unexpressed</u> antecedent when that noun has already been mentioned, or is clearly understood. The plural form **los que** / *those who* is also possible. It should be noted that this usage of **el que** often appears in proverbs and fixed expressions.

    <u>**El que**</u> **trabaja gana dinero.** / <u>The one who</u> *works earns money.*

    <u>**Los que**</u> **trabajan ganan dinero.** / <u>Those who</u> *work earn money.*

    It is possible to use the relative pronouns **quien** or **quienes** in the above structure:

    <u>**Quien**</u> **trabaja gana dinero.** / <u>He who</u> *works earns money.*

    <u>**Quienes**</u> **trabajan ganan dinero.** / <u>Those who</u> *work earn money.*

5. Use of **el cual** and **el que** after simple and compound prepositions.

    The relative pronouns **el cual** and **el que** appear after simple and compound prepositions as illustrated in the <u>nonrestrictive</u> relative clauses below. We have underlined the antecedent and the relative pronoun, and the entire relative clause.

    <u>**La mujer**, **detrás de la cual (la que)** estás sentado</u>, es mi vecina. / <u>The woman</u>, <u>behind whom you are seated</u>, is my neighbor.

    <u>**El libro** **debajo del cual (del que)** encontré mis apuntes</u> está en mi escritorio. / <u>The book</u> <u>under which I found my notes</u> is on my desk.

    <u>**Mis hermanos** **cerca de los cuales (cerca los que)** vivo</u> son simpáticos. / <u>My brothers and sisters</u> <u>near whom I live</u> are nice.

There is a tendency to use **que** after the simple prepositions **a** / *at, to,* **con** / *with,* **de** / *of, from,* and **en** / *on, at.* **El cual**, on the other hand, is generally used with the remaining simple prepositions and with compound prepositions. The following examples in <u>restrictive</u> relative clauses illustrate this.

La casa en que vivo es vieja. / *The house in which I live is old.*

El coche al lado del cual he estacionado el mío es nuevo. / *The car beside which I have parked mine is new.*

Tip
The English relative pronouns *that, which,* and *who* may be expressed by either **el cual** (**la cual, los cuales, las cuales**) and **el que** (**la que, los que, las que**) after a comma and after a preposition in Spanish. These forms, however, are considered more formal.

Exercise Set 12-3

Translate the following sentences.

1. The novel, which I am reading, is by (**de**) Gabriel García Márquez.

   _____

2. This beer, which I like a lot, is Mexican.

   _____

3. The street on which I live has no traffic.

   _____

4. This is the movie in which the actor wins a prize.

   _____

5. He who studies a lot, knows a lot.

   _____

6. Those who travel a lot are often tired.

   _____

The Possessive Relative Pronoun *Cuyo*

The possessive relative pronoun **cuyo/-a/-os/-as** / *whose* always agrees in gender (masculine, feminine) and number (singular, plural) with the noun that <u>follows</u> it. This pronoun generally appears in nonrestrictive relative clauses. We have indicated this agreement with italic typeface.

> **<u>El hombre</u>, <u>cuy*a*</u> cas*a* me gusta, vive aquí.** / *<u>The man</u>, <u>whose</u> house I like, lives here.*

It is important to note that the relative pronoun **cuyo** / *whose* in the above sentence has **el hombre** as the antecedent even though it agrees in gender and number with the following noun **casa** / *house* (*f. sg.*). When you use **cuyo** / *whose*, you always have agreement in gender and number with the <u>following noun</u>. Additional examples follow.

> **<u>Gloria</u>, <u>cuy*os*</u> hij*os* son jóvenes, es estudiante.** / *<u>Gloria</u>, <u>whose</u> children are young, is a student.*

> **<u>Alfonso</u>, <u>cuy*a*</u> cas*a* es enorme, tiene mucho dinero.** / *<u>Alfonso</u>, <u>whose</u> house is enormous, has a lot of money.*

> **<u>Mis parientes</u>, <u>cuy*os*</u> hij*os* son muy aventureros, me visitan mucho.** / *<u>My relatives</u>, <u>whose</u> children are very adventuresome, visit me a lot.*

Grammar Note

When you ask a question, you must use the phrase **¿de quién(es)?** for *whose?* as illustrated below.

> **<u>¿De quién</u> es el libro?** / *<u>Whose</u> book is it?*

> **<u>¿De quiénes</u> son estos libros?** / *<u>Whose</u> books are these?*

Exercise Set 12-4

Translate the following sentences.

1. This woman, whose dog is small, has a nice husband.

   _____

2. That man, whose daughter is married, has one granddaughter.

   _____

3. María, whose friends work in the city, has a job in the suburbs.

   _____

4. That library, whose doors are always open, has many books.

_____

5. These houses, whose windows are broken, are old.

_____

Lo que and *Lo cual*

Lo que / *what, that which* and **lo cual** / *which* are usually called neuter relative pronouns. In restrictive relative clauses, **lo que** may refer to an indefinite antecedent. Only **lo que** may begin a sentence, in which case, it refers to something previously said in a conversation.

> **Lo que me sorprende es esa mentira.** / *What (that which)* surprises me is that lie.

> **¿Ves lo que yo veo?** / *Do you see what I see?*

Lo cual / *which* and **lo que** / *which* may be used to refer to an entire preceding clause. This occurs in nonrestrictive relative clauses.

> **Mi hermana no dice nada, lo cual me molesta.** / *My sister isn't saying anything, which bothers me.*

The above sentence may also use **lo que**, as shown below.

> **Mi hermana no dice nada, lo que me molesta.** / *My sister isn't saying anything, which bothers me.*

Exercise Set 12-5

Translate the following sentences.

1. What is interesting is what she says.

_____

2. I study Spanish a lot, which is important.

_____

Exercise Set 12-6

Supply the appropriate relative pronoun in the space provided. Select from the following options: **a quien, con quien, cuyo, el cual, la cual, lo que, los cuales, que.** Use each item only once.

1. Ésta es la mujer _____ quiero.

2. _____ deseas no es posible.

3. Las personas _____ tienen una familia están contentas.

4. Elena es la persona _____ estudio.

5. Mario, _____ hijo está casado, tiene dos hijas.

6. La silla, debajo de _____ encontré la cartera, está ahí.

7. Los hombres, _____ tienen esos libros, prefieren leer.

8. El apartamento de mis amigos, _____ es muy pequeño, está allí.

USES AND FEATURES

Because of their complexity, it is worthwhile to review the uses and functions of relative pronouns. Remember that if you study them in a step-by-step fashion, it will be easy to master them. For this reason, we summarize the main points of the relative pronouns in this chapter. We indicate antecedents, relative pronouns, and relative clauses with an underline.

1. It is important to distinguish a <u>restrictive</u> relative clause from a <u>nonrestrictive</u> one. The following sentence is an example of a <u>restrictive</u> relative clause.

    <u>El hombre</u> <u>que está enfermo</u> está allá. / *<u>The man</u> <u>who is sick</u> is over there.*

    A <u>nonrestrictive</u> relative clause is set off by commas. In conversation, this is indicated by a brief pause.

    <u>La mujer</u>, <u>que vende libros</u>, prefiere leer. / *<u>The woman</u>, <u>who sells books</u>, prefers to read.*

2. The relative pronouns **quien**, **quienes** refer to people. They may be subjects or objects of prepositions.

    <u>Jorge</u>, <u>quien está enfermo</u>, no trabaja hoy. / *<u>Jorge</u>, <u>who is sick</u>, is not working today.*

    <u>Las mujeres</u> <u>a quienes veo</u> están allí. / *<u>The women</u> <u>who(m) I see</u> are there.*

3. The **el** part of the relative pronoun **el cual** changes for gender and number (**el cual, la cual, los cuales, las cuales**) and the **cual** part of **el cual** changes for number (**cual, cuales**).

    <u>Mis amigos</u>, <u>los cuales juegan al béisbol</u>, prefieren estar afuera. / *<u>My friends</u>, <u>who play baseball</u>, prefer to be outside.*

4. The **el** part of the relative pronoun **el que** changes for gender and number (**el que**, **la que**, **los que**, **las que**). The **que** part of the relative pronoun **el que**, however, is invariable (**que**).

La mesa, sobre la que puse mi libro, está allí. / *The table, on which I put my book, is there.*

5. You may use the neuter relative pronouns **lo que** / *that which* and **lo cual** / *that which* to refer to an indefinite antecedent or previously discussed notions. **Lo que** may begin a sentence.

Lo que dices es interesante. / *What (that which) you say is interesting.*

Hago todo el trabajo, lo cual no te importa. / *I do all the work, which doesn't matter to you.*

6. The possessive relative pronoun **cuyo/-a/-os/-as** / *whose* always agrees with the noun that follows it.

Mis amigos cuyo trabajo es difícil viven en la ciudad. / *My friends whose work is difficult live in the city.*

Mi hermano cuya esposa es abogada vive en Los Angeles. / *My brother whose wife is a lawyer lives in Los Angeles.*

Review of Section 1 (Pronouns)

(Chapters 1–12)

Review Exercise Set 1-1

A. Use the appropriate form for the English word you (**tú, Ud.**, **vosotros/-as, Uds.**) according to the context.

1. Teresa, _____

2. Señores, _____ (Latin America)

3. Jorge y Carmen, _____ (Spain)

4. Estimados profesores, _____ (Spain and Latin America)

5. Amigos, _____ (Latin America)

B. Supply the appropriate verbal ending in Spanish for the following **-ar, -er,** and **-ir** verbs to correspond with the subject provided.

1. ella habl_____

2. nosotras beb_____

3. Uds. escrib_____

4. tú compr_____

5. vosotros viv_____

6. Ud. cant_____

7. Yo le_____

8. él estudi_____

C. Translate the following sentences into Spanish. Be careful about the English word *it*.

1. It is possible.

_____

2. It is late.

_____

3. It is here.

_____

4. It is raining.

_____

5. It is a book.

_____

Review Exercise Set 1-2

Use one of the following interrogative pronouns in each blank: **¿qué?**, **¿quién?**, **¿quiénes?**, **¿cuál?**, **¿cuáles?**. Use each one only once.

1. ¿_____ de los dos quieres?

2. ¿_____ están aquí?

3. ¿_____ es ella?

4. ¿_____ es esto?

5. ¿_____ son las capitales de Sudamérica?

Review Exercise Set 1-3

Use one of the following words in each blank according to the context: **yo, mí, conmigo, tú, ti, contigo, consigo, Ud**. Use each one only once.

1. Él trae los libros _____.

2. Según (*me*) _____, es correcto.

3. ¿Quieres venir _____?

4. Excepto _____, todos mis amigos van a la playa.

5. Teresa, el libro es para _____ (*fam. sg.*).

6. Voy _____.

7. El regalo es para _____ (*me*).

8. Ella va con _____ (*pol. sg.*)

Review Exercise Set 1-4
Replace the direct objects with direct object pronouns. Remember that there are two options with infinitives and with present participles (gerunds). In these cases, write both possibilities.

1. Julio lee el periódico.

   _____

2. Voy a estudiar la lección.

   _____

   _____

3. Estoy escribiendo la carta.

   _____

   _____

Review Exercise Set 1-5
A. Translate the following sentences. Use indirect object pronouns in your answers. Remember to use the redundant indirect object pronoun in the third person singular and plural. If there are two ways of writing an answer, please do so.

1. I write the letter to her.

   _____

2. He wants to give them (*m.*) the book.

   _____

   _____

3. He is not selling the car to his girlfriend.

   _____

   _____

B. Translate the following sentences. Remember the Spanish format for **gustar** / *to be pleasing to* verbs and related verbs.

1. I like Chile.

_____

2. He likes to swim.

_____

3. We do not like soap operas.

_____

4. I am attracted to you (*fam. sg.*).

_____

5. I like you (*fam. sg.*)

_____

Review Exercise Set 1-6

Replace the indirect and direct objects with indirect and direct object pronouns, that is, with double object pronouns. If there are two ways of writing an answer, please do so. Remember the order of the pronouns (indirect object pronoun + direct object pronoun). Remember also the redundant indirect object pronoun in the third person singular and plural.

1. Miguel les muestra la casa a sus amigos.

_____

2. Raúl va a cantarle la canción a Irene.

_____

_____

3. Estoy entregándole los libros a los estudiantes.

_____

_____

Review Exercise Set 1-7

Translate the following sentences.

1. They go to bed late.

   _____

2. We embrace one another.

   _____

3. I dress my child (*m.*).

   _____

4. I dress myself (*m.*).

   _____

5. They see themselves.

   _____

Review Exercise Set 1-8

Translate the following sentences into Spanish (use the **se** passive).

1. Spanish is spoken here.

   _____

2. The president is elected in November.

   _____

3. Cars are sold here.

   _____

Translate the following sentences into Spanish (use the impersonal **se**).

1. They say that it is here.

   _____

2. One enters here.

   _____

3. People know the truth.

   _____

Review Exercise Set 1-9

Translate the following sentences. Remember agreement in number (*sg.*, *pl.*) and gender (*m.*, *f.*) for the possessive pronouns. When there is ambiguity, express the possessive in two ways (possessive pronoun and **de** + prepositional pronoun).

1. I have my notebook and they have theirs.

   _____

   _____

2. This book is ours.

   _____

   _____

3. My family lives in Venezuela, but hers lives in Spain.

   _____

   _____

4. My sister is blond and hers is brunette.

   _____

   _____

Review Exercise Set 1-10

Translate the following sentences.

1. This short story is more interesting than that one (nearby).

   _____

2. That (at a distance) mountain is taller than this one.

   _____

3. This is terrible!

   _____

4. These books are easy and those (over there) are hard.

   _____

5. This house is mine and that one (nearby) is Pedro's (use **de**).

   _____

Review Exercise Set 1-11

Translate the following sentences.

1. I have the old house and she has the new one.

   _____

2. What's mine is yours (*fam. sg.*)

   _____

3. The first woman is my wife and the second one is Marco's (use **de**).

   _____

4. I have two hundred books, but Pilar has three hundred.

   _____

5. Do you (*fam. sg.*) see someone?

   _____

6. I see no one.

   _____

7. Do you see something?

   _____

8. I see nothing.

   _____

9. I have several (*masc.*).

   _____

10. They read many (*fem. pl.*).

   _____

Review Exercise Set 1-12

Supply the appropriate relative pronoun in the space provided. Select from the following options: **con quien**, **cuyo**, **la cual**, **las cuales**, **lo que**, **que**, **quien**. Use each pronoun only once.

1. _____ buscas no está aquí.

2. Esa casa, al lado de _____ está la mía, es nueva.

3. Emilio es la persona _____ trabajo.

4. Claudia, _____ hijo estudia en la universidad, trabaja conmigo.

5. La novela, de _____ hablé ayer, se vende en esa librería.

6. Las amigas de Claudio, _____ están enfermas, no trabajan hoy.

7. _____ trabaja mucho, gana mucho.

Section 2

WHAT IS A PREPOSITION?

A preposition is a part of speech that expresses or describes a relationship between two words in a sentence. The word preposition literally means something that is "put before." In this instance, this part of speech is placed in a position <u>before</u> some other word, and that word is usually a noun or a noun phrase.

A preposition in combination with another word or phrase, for example, a noun or a noun phrase, creates a **prepositional phrase**. The following are some examples of prepositional phrases in English. We have placed the preposition in **boldface** type and we have <u>underlined</u> the entire prepositional phrase.

<u>**at** the office</u>
<u>**in** the kitchen</u>
<u>**with** my friends</u>
<u>**from** the terrace</u>
<u>**around** the corner</u>
<u>**next to** my home</u>
<u>**on top of** the table</u>
<u>**on the side of** the bed</u>

You can see that prepositions in English may be simple (one word) or compound (two or more words). All of the above prepositions indicate **location**. In very general terms, it is possible to speak of "meaning classes" of prepositions, that is, prepositions that possess a broad meaning such as the one we have just mentioned (location). There are two other broad categories of meaning for prepositions: motion and movement, and time.

The following examples illustrate prepositions with the general meaning of **motion and movement**. All are prepositional phrases. We have placed the preposition in **boldface** type and we have <u>underlined</u> the entire prepositional phrase.

<u>**toward** the building</u>
<u>**along** the highway</u>
<u>**around** the block</u>

The following additional prepositional phrases illustrate the general meaning of **time**.

<u>**after** the party</u>
<u>**until** tomorrow</u>
<u>**before** noon</u>

We will examine all three of these general semantic categories of prepositions in the first chapter of this section of the book, namely, location, motion and movement, and time.

The following brief paragraph illustrates how common and frequent prepositions are in English. We have indicated in **boldface** type each preposition.

I woke up early because I had to go **to** work **for** an important meeting **about** a business matter. Once I got **to** the office. I met **with** my colleagues **in front of** the main office. **Before** the start **of** the meeting, I spoke **with** my associates. We all went **into** the room and we sat **at** a large oval desk. The head **of** the department gave an agenda **to** each **of** us. **After** a long discussion, we decided **on** a plan **of** action.

It should be noted that there are certain prepositions that we will address individually because of their frequency of occurrence, namely, **a** / *to, at*, **con** / *with*, **de** / *of, from*, and **en** / *at, in*. We will also look at prepositions according to their meaning class (location, motion and movement, time). In the second chapter of Section Two, we shall examine the two problematic prepositions **para** and **por**, both with a basic meaning in English of *for*. In the third chapter of this Section we shall examine verbs and adjectives with "characteristic" prepositions, that is, prepositions that must occur with these two parts of speech when there is a following noun or infinitive (the form of the verb that ends in **-r**).

In the index of many reference books and pedagogical textbooks, prepositions are listed individually so that you have to look for them throughout these books. Although a few such works have a chapter or a section devoted to prepositions, it is relatively rare to be able to locate them all in one place. This haphazard approach to the discussion of prepositions makes it difficult to master them. What we intend to do in this section is discuss them all at once and in a comprehensible and systematic way.

1

Prepositions

In the introduction, we pointed out that a preposition may be a single word (<u>simple</u> preposition) such as **a** / *to/at*, or **en** / *on*, and so forth. It may also consist of two, three, or even four words (<u>compound</u> preposition) such as **delante de** / *in front of* or **al lado de** / *next to*, and **a la derecha de** / *to the right of.* We provide examples of each type below. You will note that we also include the prepositions **para** / *for* and **por** / *for.* Both have an English meaning of *for*, but their usage requires a more detailed discussion, and you will find it in the next chapter.

As a point of departure, we include here a typical enumeration of simple prepositions and compound prepositions.

SOME COMMON SIMPLE PREPOSITIONS

a	*at, on*
ante	*before, in the presence of*
bajo	*under*
con	*with*
contra	*against*
de	*from, of*
desde	*from, since*
durante	*during*
en	*on, in*
entre	*between, among*
excepto	*except*
hacia	*toward*
hasta	*until, up to*
incluso	*including*
menos	*except*
para	*for*
por	*for*
salvo	*except, save*
según	*according to*
sin	*without*
sobre	*upon, on, above, around*
tras	*behind*

SOME COMMON COMPOUND PREPOSITIONS

a la derecha de	*to the right of*
a la izquierda de	*to the left of*
a través de	*across, through*
acerca de	*about, concerning*
además de	*besides*
al lado de	*beside*
alrededor de	*around*
antes de	*before*
cerca de	*near*
debajo de	*beneath*
delante de	*in front of*
dentro de	*inside of*
encima de	*on top of*
enfrente de	*in front of, facing*
fuera de	*outside, except*
junto a	*next to, near*
lejos de	*far from*

Grammar Note

After any preposition, you **always** use the infinitive form of the verb (the verb form that ends in **-r**) as illustrated below.

Antes de entrar en la biblioteca, comí. / *Upon entering the library, I ate.*

Después de hacer la tarea, usé mi teléfono celular. / *After doing the chore, I used my cell phone.*

Four Common Spanish Prepositions

In this first part of the chapter, we shall examine the most common prepositions in Spanish to learn something about their usage. Later, we shall examine Spanish prepositions according to their basic meanings: location, motion and movement, time. We devote the entire next chapter to two additional common Spanish prepositions, namely, **para** and **por**, both of which have *for* as one of their meanings.

Four of the most common prepositions that we will consider here are **a** / *to, at,* **con** / *with,* **de** / *of, from,* and **en** / *on, in.*

a / *to, at*

The preposition **a** has various uses as indicated below.

1. To indicate the meaning of *to* or *for* before an indirect object.

    Le doy el libro a Juan. / *I give the book to Juan.*
    Le hago el café a María. / *I make the coffee for María.*

2. To indicate a point in time. It frequently corresponds to the English preposition *at*.

    La telenovela empieza a las ocho de la noche. / *The soap opera begins at 8 P.M.*
    Bebo café a la medianoche / I drink coffee at midnight.

3. To indicate measurement and prices.

    Conduje a cien kilómetros por hora ayer. / *I drove at 100 kilometers per hour yesterday.*
    ¿A cuánto se vende? / *How much does it sell for?*

4. To indicate movement or direction after certain verbs (see Chapter 3 of this Section for more about verbs with characteristic prepositions). With these verbs and adjectives, the Spanish word **a** may be rendered with another preposition or none at all.

    Llego a la oficina temprano. / *I arrive at the office early.*
    Vengo a clase tarde. / *I come to class late.*
    Voy a casa. / *I go home.*

5. To indicate that the following noun or noun phrase is a direct object of the main verb (see Grammar Note on personal **a**, page 127). In English, there is no corresponding word, so you must make a conscious effort to remember to insert the personal **a**. Remember that some verbs (**buscar** / *to look for*, **mirar** / *to look at*, **esperar** / *to wait for*) have an intrinsic preposition in English. For this reason, it is not necessary to use any preposition when these verbs are followed by a noun that refers to an object. The personal **a** is only necessary before a direct object that refers to a person.

    Veo a mis padres. / *I see my parents.*
    Conozco a tu abuelo. / *I know your grandfather.*
    Busco a mi amiga. / *I look for my (female) friend.*
    Miro a Carmen. / *I look at Carmen.*

6. With the definite article **el** / *the* to create the contraction **al** / *upon* (see Grammar Note, page 127). **Al** is always used with an infinitive (**-r** form of the verb). Sometimes it is possible to render this usage with a phrase with the word *when* and a conjugated verb.

    Al despertarme, fui a la cocina. / *Upon waking up, I went to the kitchen.*
    Al entrar en el edificio, vi el ascensor. / *Upon entering the building, I saw the elevator / When I entered the building, I saw the elevator.*

7. To express certain idiomatic expressions. The meaning of **a** in these expressions varies (*at, by, in, on, to*).

a casa	*at home*	**a** oscuras	*in the dark*
a ciegas	*blindly*	**a** pie	*on foot*
a fondo	*thoroughly*	**a** propósito	*on purpose*
a lo mejor	*probably*	**a** sabiendas	*knowingly*
a la derecha	*to the right*	**a** tiempo	*on time*
a la fuerza	*against one's will*	**a** veces	*at times*
a la izquierda	*to the left*	gota **a** gota	*drop by drop*
a lo loco	*in a crazy fashion*	paso **a** paso	*step by step*
a mano	by hand	poco **a** poco	*little by little*
a menudo	*often*	uno **a** uno	*one by one*

Exercise Set 1-1

Translate the following sentences into Spanish.

1. He arrives home on time.

    _____

2. They (*m.*) see the children.

    _____

3. I send the email to my sister.

    _____

4. Upon seeing the accident, I called the police.

    _____

5. They (*m.*) sell the fruit at one hundred pesos a pound.

    _____

6. I get up at eight.

    _____

7. Little by little, I am learning Spanish.

    _____

8. They (*m.*) go to the bookstore often.

    _____

Grammar Note

In Spanish, when the direct object (the recipient of the action of the verb) refers to a person or persons, you must place the "personal **a**" immediately before the direct object. There is no such form in English, so you should remember to place it there. The following examples illustrate the "personal **a**."

Quiero a Rosa. / *I love Rosa.*
Veo a mi amigo. / *I see my friend.*

If there is a series of names, you must place the "personal **a**" before each name:

Veo a Margarita y a Jesús. / *I see Margarita and Jesús.*

If you ask a question with **¿quién?** / *whom?* (sg.) or **¿quiénes?** / *whom?* (pl.), when it is a direct object, you must use the "personal **a**" as seen in the following examples.

¿A quién ves? / *Who(m) do you see?*
¿A quiénes admiras? / *Who(m) do you admire?*

You can even use the "personal **a**" with your pets.

Quiero a mi perro. / I *love my dog.*

You use the "personal **a**" with the following verbs that have an implicit preposition.

Miro a Juan. / *I look at John.*
Buscas a Magadalena. / *You are looking for Magdalena.*
Uds. esperan a Jorge. / *You are waiting for Jorge.*

Finally, you do not use the "personal **a**" with the verbs **ser** / *to be*, **tener** / *to have*, and **hay** / *there is, there are:*

Alba es doctora. / *Alba is a doctor.*
Tengo tres hermanos. / *I have three brothers.*
Hay muchos estudiantes aquí. / *There are many students here.*

Grammar Note

When you use the preposition **a** / *to* with the masculine singular definite article **el** / *the*, these two words contract to **al** / *to the*, as shown below.

Voy <u>al</u> parque. / *I'm going to the park.*
Voy <u>al</u> centro. / *I'm going downtown.*

Con / *with*

The second frequently used preposition in Spanish is **con** / *with*. It has the following uses.

1. To indicate accompaniment.

    Voy a la fiesta <u>con</u> Esmeralda. / *I'm going to the party <u>with</u> Esmeralda.*
    Rosa está <u>con</u> sus padres. / *Rosa is <u>with</u> her parents.*

2. To indicate the means by which something is achieved.

    Ella trabaja <u>con</u> la mente. / *She works <u>with</u> her mind.*

3. To create adverbial expressions of manner with nouns.

    Ellos estudian la lección <u>con cuidado</u>. / *They study the lesson <u>carefully</u>.*
    Leí la novela <u>con dificultad</u>. / *I read the novel <u>with difficulty</u>.*

4. After certain verbs. (See Chapter 3 of this Section for more about verbs with characteristic prepositions.) Using these verbs and adjectives, the Spanish word **con** may be rendered with another preposition or none at all.

    Me junto <u>con</u> ellos. / *I join <u>with</u> them.*
    Cuento <u>con</u> mis amigos. / *I count <u>on</u> my friends.*
    Ella se casa <u>con</u> Antonio. / *She marries Antonio.*

Prepositional Pronouns with *Con*

When used with prepositional pronouns, the preposition **con** / *with* has some special forms in the first, second, and third person singular, and third person plural as illustrated below (see also Section 1, Chapter 3).

Singular		Plural	
1st person	<u>**conmigo**</u> /*with me*	1st person	**con nosotros** / *with us (m.)* **con nosotras** / *with us (f.)*
2nd person	**contigo** / *you (fam. sg)*	2nd person	**con vosotros** / *with you (fam. pl., m.)* **con vosotras** / *with you (fam. pl., f.)*
3rd person	<u>**consigo**</u> *with him, with her, with you (pol. sg.)* and **con él** / *with him* **con ella** / *with her* **con Ud.** / *with you (pol. sg.)* **con ello** / *with it (neuter)*	3rd person	<u>**consigo**</u> / *with them with you (pol. pl.)* and **con ellos** / *with them (m.)* **con ellas** / *with them (f.)* **con Uds.** / *with you (pol. pl.)*

In the first and second person singular, you use the forms **conmigo** / *with me,* and **contigo** / *with you.*

> **Esmeralda baila <u>conmigo</u>**. / **Esmeralda is dancing <u>with me</u>.**
> **Voy al concierto <u>contigo</u>**. / **I am going to the concert <u>with you</u>.**

In the third person singular and plural, the form **consigo** / *with him, with her, with you* (*pol. sg.*), *with them, with you* (*pol. pl.*) is used when the reference is to the subject of the sentence, as illustrated below.

> **Andrés trae los libros <u>consigo</u>**. / *Andrés brings the books <u>with him</u>.*
> **Elvira lleva el paraguas <u>consigo</u>**. / *Elvira carries the umbrella <u>with her</u>.*

Compare the above sentences with the following, where the prepositional pronoun does not refer to the subject.

> **Ana y Luis son estudiantes y ella tiene clases <u>con él</u>**. / *Ana and Luis are students and she has classes <u>with him</u>.*

Exercise Set 1-2
Translate the following sentences.

1. He speaks Spanish with a foreign accent.

   _____

2. They (*m.*) are going with me.

   _____

3. I dream about my wife.

   _____

4. He is bringing the work with him.

   _____

5. I am with my grandmother.

   _____

6. She has an appointment with him tomorrow.

   _____

7. They (*m.*) count on you (*fam. sg.*).

   _____

8. They (*m.*) arrive in a hurry.

   _____

de / *of, from*

A third frequently used preposition in Spanish is **de** / *of.* It has the following uses.

1. To indicate place of origin.

    Ignacio es <u>de</u> Madrid. / *Ignacio is <u>from</u> Madrid.*
    Mi amiga <u>de</u> Santiago está aquí. / *My friend <u>from</u> Santiago is here.*

2. To indicate possession. Remember that there is no **'s** (*apostrophe s*) in Spanish.

    ¿<u>De</u> quién es el libro? / <u>*Whose*</u> *book is it?*
    El libro es <u>de</u> Amparo. / *The book is <u>Amparo's</u>.*

3. To indicate composition (what something is made of).

    ¿<u>De</u> qué es esta casa? / *What is this house made <u>of</u>?*
    Esta casa es <u>de</u> madera. / *This house is made <u>of</u> wood.*

4. To specify the contents of a container.

    Una botella <u>de</u> agua / *a bottle <u>of</u> water*
    Una copa <u>de</u> vino / *a glass <u>of</u> wine*

5. To indicate exact time of the day or a date.

    Es la una <u>de</u> la tarde. / *It's one P.M.*
    Son las nueve <u>de</u> la mañana. / *It's nine A.M.*
    Son las once <u>de</u> la noche. / *It's eleven P.M.*
    Es el primero <u>de</u> noviembre. / *It's the first <u>of</u> November.*
    Es el veintidós <u>de</u> enero. / *It's the twenty second <u>of</u> January.*

6. After certain verbs. (See Chapter 3 of this Section for more about verbs with characteristic prepositions.) Using these verbs, the Spanish word **de** may be rendered with another preposition or none at all.

    Me burlo <u>de</u> mis parientes. / *I make fun <u>of</u> my relatives.*
    Tomás sirve <u>de</u> guía. / *Tomás serves <u>as</u> a guide.*
    Ceso <u>de</u> fumar. / *I stop smoking.*

7. To indicate certain idiomatic expressions.

<u>de</u> balde	*for free*
<u>de</u> buen humor	*in a good mood*
<u>de</u> buena gana	*willingly*
<u>de</u> gratis	*for free*
<u>de</u> mal humor	*in a bad mood*
<u>de</u> mala gana	*unwillingly*
<u>de</u> memoria	*by heart*
<u>de</u> nada	*you're welcome*
<u>de</u> nuevo	*again*
<u>de</u> pie	*standing up*
<u>de</u> prisa	*in a hurry*
<u>de</u> puntillas	*on tiptoe*

<u>de</u> repente	*suddenly*
<u>de</u> rodillas	*on one's knees*
<u>de</u> veras	*really*
<u>de</u> vez en cuando	*from time to time*

Grammar Note

Note that the preposition **de** / *of* and the masculine singular definite article **el** / *the* contract to the single form **del** / *of the* in Spanish, as shown below.

¿De quién es el libro? / *Whose it book is it?*
El libro es del hombre. / *It's the man's book.*

Exercise Set 1-3

Translate the following sentences.

1. It's March 28th.

   _____

2. The pen is metal (use **de**).

   _____

3. My relatives are from Bolivia.

   _____

4. She gets tired of studying prepositions.

   _____

5. It's 3 P.M.

   _____

6. It's Mario's (use **de**) car.

   _____

7. He wants a cup of coffee.

   _____

8. I learn the prepositions by heart.

   _____

en / at, on, in

The last of the four frequently used prepositions in Spanish is **en** / *at, on, in.* It has the following uses.

1. To indicate a location in space.

    Prefiero estar en la universidad. / *I prefer to be at the university.*
    El libro está en la mesa. / *The book is on the table.*

2. To indicate means of transportation. Note that you can also use **por** / *by* with these expressions (see the following chapter for more on the uses of **por**).

    Voy en avión. / *I'm going by plane.*
    Voy en tren. / *I'm going by train.*

3. To indicate when something takes place.

    En junio fui a España. / *In June, I went to Spain.*
    Estudiaré en una hora. / *I will study in an hour.*

4. After certain verbs. (See Chapter 3 of this Section for more about verbs with characteristic prepositions.) Using these verbs, the Spanish word **en** may be rendered with another preposition or none at all.

    Insisto en hablar con Elena. / *I insist on speaking with Elena.*
    Confío en mis amigos. / *I trust my friends.*

5. In certain idiomatic expressions.

en cambio	*on the other hand*
en casa	*at home*
en lugar de	*in place of*
en punto	*sharp, on the dot*
en seguida	*at once*
en vez de	*instead of*

Exercise Set 1-4

Translate the following sentences.

1. We think about going to the library.

_____

2. They (*m.*) travel by train.

_____

3. In summer, I swim a lot.

_____

4. I have an exam in four days.

_____

5. I notice the woman.

_____

6. It's five o'clock sharp.

_____

Exercise Set 1-5
In the following sentences, use <u>one</u> of the following five prepositions: **a, al, con, de, en** according to the context.

1. Mi amigo es _____ Arizona.

2. _____ recibir mi nota, grité.

3. Estudio _____ otros estudiantes.

4. Mi gato está _____ la mesa.

5. Miro _____ mi prima.

6. Siempre viajo _____ avión.

7. Son las ocho _____ la mañana.

8. Lo hago _____ mano.

9. Se venden _____ cincuenta pesos.

10. La casa es _____ Soledad.

MEANING CLASSES OF PREPOSITIONS
When thinking of prepositions, it is useful to categorize them according to their meaning rather their form. We have noted that prepositions may belong to very general semantic categories that are called "meaning classes," that is, prepositions that have a basic meaning of 1. Location, 2. Motion and movement, 3. Time.

Prepositions That Refer to Location

Prepositions that refer to location or situation are both simple and compound. When you use the English verb *to be* with prepositions that refer to location, you must use the verb **estar** / *to be*. The following sentences illustrate some of the prepositions of location in Spanish.

a la derecha de	*to the right of*
a la izquierda de	*to the left of*
a través de	*across, through*
al lado de	*beside*
cerca de	*near*
con	*with*
debajo de	*beneath*
delante de	*in front of*
dentro de	*inside*
en	*in, on*
encima de	*on top of*
enfrente de	*in front of, facing*
fuera de	*outside, except*
junto a	*next to, near*
lejos de	*far from*
sobre	*above*

The following prepositions refer to geographical location. They are useful for asking and giving directions.

al norte de	*to the north of*
al este de	*to the east of*
al oeste de	*to the west of*
al sur de	*to the south of*
al noreste de	*to the northeast of*
al noroeste de	*to the northwest of*
al sureste de (al sudeste de)	*to the southeast of*
al suroeste de (al sudoeste de)	*to the southwest of*

Exercise Set 1-6

Translate the following sentences.

1. Isabel is to the right of Bernardo.

_____

2. Portugal is to the west of Spain.

_____

3. The books are next to the desk.

4. We are near the main plaza.

5. Next to the bookstore, there is a park.

6. She is in front of the class today.

7. The house is inside the city.

8. Facing him is the stadium.

Motion and Movement Prepositions

Prepositions that refer to motion and movement are both simple and compound. See the following chapter on **para** and **por** for more.

When you use the English verb *to be* with prepositions that refer to motion and movement, you must use the verb **estar** / *to be*. The following sentences illustrate some of the prepositions of motion and movement in Spanish.

a	*to*
a lo largo de	*along*
alrededor de	*around*
hacia	*toward*
más allá de	*beyond*
por	*through, along*

Exercise Set 1-7

Translate the following sentences.

1. Along the highway, there are many interesting sites.

2. You (*fam. sg.*) must go beyond the mountains.

3. I took a walk around the plaza yesterday.

4. Beatriz is traveling toward Barcelona.

    _____

5. I go to the country often.

    _____

6. He runs through the park.

    _____

Prepositions That Refer to Time

The following list includes some common simple and compound prepositions that refer to time. For more on **para** and **por**, see the next chapter.

antes de	*before*
desde	*since*
después de	*after*
durante	*during*
hasta	*until*
por	*during, in*

Note
In English, the prepositions *before* and *after* may refer to time or location. Spanish uses different prepositions to express these two meanings. **Antes de** / *before* and **después de** / *after* refer to time, while **delante de** / *before* and **detrás de** / *after* refer to location.   **<u>Antes de</u> acostarme, leí el periódico.** / <u>Before</u> going to bed, I read the newspaper.   **Después de ir a casa, bebí café.** / <u>After</u> going home, I drank coffee.   **El niño está <u>detrás de</u> la cerca.** / The child stands <u>after</u> the fence.   **El gato está <u>delante de</u> la cama.** / The cat stands <u>before</u> the bed.

Exercise Set 1-8

Translate the following sentences.

1. I eat before going to the office.

    _____

2. I felt sick since yesterday.

    _____

3. During the afternoon, I drink coffee.

    _____

4. After reading the newspaper, I go to the office.

_____

5. I am going to study until 8.

_____

6. In the morning, I take a walk.

_____

Six Exceptional Prepositions

The following six prepositions are exceptional in that they take a subject pronoun rather than an object pronoun (see Chapter 3). In all other ways, however, they are just like the other simple prepositions.

entre	*between*
excepto	*except*
incluso	*including*
menos	*except*
salvo	*except*
según	*according to*

When you use these prepositions, you must note the following exceptional usage.

entre tú y yo / *between you and me*
según yo / *according to me*
según tú / *according to you*
excepto yo / *except me*
salvo tú / *except you*
menos yo / *except me*
incluso tú / *including you*

Exercise Set 1-9
Give the Spanish version for the following.

1. according to you (*fam. sg.*) _____

2. including me _____

3. except me _____

4. between him and me _____

5. according to you (*pol. sg.*) _____

6. including us _____

USES AND FEATURES

1. Traditional grammars classify prepositions as simple (one word), for example, **a** / *at, to,* or compound (more than one word), for example, **al lado de** / *beside.*

2. Some verbs in Spanish have inherent prepositions, that is, the preposition is in the meaning of the verb itself. Some common examples follow.

   buscar / *to look for*
   esperar / *to wait for*
   mirar / *to look at*

3. Four commonly used prepositions, **a**, **con**, **de**, **en**, require individual discussion. They may be used with in idiomatic expressions and after certain verbs (see Section II, Chapter 3 for discussion).

4. In general, it is possible to categorize Spanish prepositions according to meaning class, or a common shared meaning. There are three basic meaning classes of prepositions: location, motion and movement, and time. The following are some examples.

   Location: cerca de / *near,* **lejos de** / *far,* **encima de** / *on top of,* and so forth.

   Motion and movement: a / *to,* **hacia** / *toward,* and so forth.

   Time: **antes de** / *before,* **depués de** / *after,* and so forth.

5. There are six exceptional prepositions that take subject pronouns rather than prepositional pronouns: **entre** / *between,* **excepto** / *except,* **incluso** / *including,* **menos** / *except,* **salvo** / *except,* and **según** / *according to.*

2

Para and *Por*

Spanish has two prepositions with the basic meaning of *for*. They are **para** and **por**. Students of Spanish are sometimes perplexed about when to use these two prepositions. If you learn their uses in a step-by-step fashion, you will find that they are not as puzzling as you may think.

The Latin word origins of both **para** and **por** provide a clue to their present-day meaning. Spanish **para** is derived from a combination of two Latin prepositions: **pro** and **ad**. **Pro** has a general meaning of *forward*. **Ad** means *to* or *towards*. Thus, the amalgamation of **pro** and **ad** into the Spanish **para** created a new preposition with the general meaning of "goal" or "destination."

Spanish **por**, on the other hand, is a combination preposition that joined the meanings of the two Latin prepositions **per** and **pro**. The Latin **per** has many meanings, including *because of, on account of, through, with, by, by means of, along, over, throughout, during, in the course of.* **Pro** means *in front of, before, on behalf of, in return for, instead of, for, as.* This multiplicity of meanings continued on in the Spanish preposition **por**.

In order to determine which one of these two prepositions you need to use, you should think about what you want to say. In a very general sense, **para** has the meaning of destination, while **por** has the general sense of source. When you are beginning to learn to use these two prepositions, it is helpful to consider very carefully what you mean. This may seem to be a bit tedious at first, but it will ultimately yield positive results after you complete this chapter.

PARA

Para has the fewest number of meanings and uses. Again, remember that **para** has the general meaning of destination. This notion may be represented as $X \rightarrow Y$, that is, someone or something moves to, or is transferred to someone else or some other place.

Para has the following five basic meanings: (1) purpose; (2) motion toward a destination or goal; (3) time limit or a specific point in time; (4) implied comparison; and (5) personal opinion. We will now examine each one of these meanings with selected examples of their usage. We indicate in brackets [ ] the meaning of **para** in each context.

Uses of *Para*

1. **Purpose.** When you want to indicate what something is used for, you use the preposition **para** + an infinitive (the form of the verb ending in **-r**).

   Este libro es para entender los pronombres y las preposiciones en español. / *This book is to understand pronouns and prepositions in Spanish.* [**for the purpose of**]
   El bolígrafo y el cuaderno son para apuntar. / *The pen and notebook are for taking notes.* [**for the purpose of**]
   La mochila es para llevar los libros. / *A backpack is for carrying books.* [**for the purpose of**]

   A related meaning of **para** is *in order to* followed by an infinitive (the form of the verb ending in **-r**).

   Para trabajar, él viaja mucho. / *In order to work, he travels a lot.* [**in order to**]
   Para vivir, como y bebo. / *In order to live, I eat and drink.* [**in order to**]
   Para saber más, escucho mucho. / *In order to know more, I listen a lot.* [**in order to**]

   Para may indicate use and suitability in the sense of ultimate purpose.

   una copa para vino / *a wine glass* [**for**]
   un vaso para leche / *a milk glass* [**for**]
   un estante para libros / *a shelf for books* [**for**]

2. **Motion toward a destination or goal.** One of the basic meanings of **para** is the movement of a person or a thing toward a specific destination ($X \rightarrow Y$).

   Use **para** to indicate final destination:

   Mis padres parten para Montevideo. / *My parents are leaving for Montevideo.* [**destination**]
   Parto para la universidad. / *I'm leaving for the university.* [**destination**]
   Este libro es para Lidia. / *This book is for Lidia.* [**destination**]

   Para may mean the final purpose or goal of an action or set of actions:

   Mi amiga estudia para doctora. / *My girlfriend is studying to become a doctor.* [**in order to become**]
   Se prepara para abogado. / *He is preparing himself to be a lawyer.* [**in order to become**]
   Mi hermana estudia para ingeniera. / *My sister is study to become an engineer.* [**in order to become**]

3. **Time limit or a specific point in time.** You may use **para** to specify a temporal goal or endpoint.

   Para mañana, ¡lean el capítulo 2! / *For tomorrow, read Chapter 2!* [**by a certain time**]
   Para octubre, tenemos que terminar esta tarea. / *By October, we have to finish this task.* [**by a certain time**]
   Para el fin del año, debemos pagar la deuda. / *By the end of the year, we must pay the debt.* [**by a certain time**]

4. **Comparison. Para** may introduce an implied comparison. In this usage, it may have the meaning of *considering that*.

Para niño, comprende mucho. / *For a child, he understands a lot.* [**considering that**]

Para un adulto, no se comporta bien. / *For an adult, he doesn't behave well.* [**considering that**]

Para un profesor, prefiere mirar la televisión. / *For a professor, he prefers to* watch TV. [**considering that**]

5. **Personal opinion.** You may use **para** to indicate a personal opinion.

Para mí, tu comportamiento no es aceptable. / *As for me, your behavior is not acceptable.* [**in my opinion**]

Para mi amigo, es importante trabajar mucho. / *As for my friend, it is important to work a lot.* [**in my friend's opinion**]

Para ellos, esta persona es bien conocida. / *As for them, this person is well known.* [**in their opinion**]

Exercise Set 2-1

A. Translate the following sentences.

1. By next week, I must do this assignment.

   _____

2. For an adolescent (*f.*), she studies a lot.

   _____

3. This wine cup is mine.

   _____

4. These gifts are for Beatriz.

   _____

5. I leave for Salamanca tomorrow.

   _____

6. In order be in Lima, I must leave early.

   _____

7. In my opinion, it is late.

   _____

8. She is studying to be a nurse.

   _____

9. I have to be there by Friday.

   _____

10. We are going to buy a car for Enrique.

_____

11. This book is for learning pronouns and prepositions.

_____

B. Write as briefly as possible the reason for the use of **para** in each of the following sentences in the space provided. Refer to the previous discussion on the uses and meanings of **para**.

1. Los lápices se usan <u>para</u> escribir. _____

2. Mi hija estudia <u>para</u> abogada. _____

3. <u>Para</u> él, lo importante es decir la verdad. _____

4. El coche es <u>para</u> María. _____

5. <u>Para</u> mis estudiantes, este examen es fácil. _____

6. <u>Para</u> el fin del mes, debes pagar la cuenta. _____

7. Esta medicina es <u>para</u> un dolor de garganta. _____

8. <u>Para</u> agosto, hace fresco. _____

9. <u>Para</u> mí, no hay otra posibilidad. _____

10. ¿<u>Para</u> quién es el regalo? _____

11. Esta bebida no es <u>para</u> niños. _____

POR

Por is the preposition that has the largest number of potential meanings. The multiple meanings of **por** in the examples below reflect the original Latin meanings of the two prepositions (**per**, **pro**) from which it derives. Again, remember that the basic meaning of **por** is source in the sense of motivation or rationale.

Por has the following basic meanings: (1) motivation; (2) emotion; (3) object of an errand after certain verbs of motion; (4) approximate location, space, or time; (5) duration of an action or time; (6) substitution and exchange; (7) multiplication, rate, and unit of measure; (8) means, manner, and agent; (9) idiomatic and fixed expressions; and (10) idiomatic usage with **estar** / *to be* ("*to be about to*"). We will now examine each one of these meanings with selected examples of their usage. We indicate in brackets [ ] the meaning of **por** in each context.

Uses of *Por*

1. **Motivation.**

   Él es soldado <u>por</u> ser patriótico. / *He is a soldier because he is patriotic.* [**because**]
   Me casé con ella <u>por</u> amor. / *I married her out of love.* [**out of**]
   Lo hago todo <u>por</u> mis hijos. / *I do everything for my children.* [**on behalf of**]

2. **Emotion.**

   Su odio <u>por</u> aquel hombre era increíble / *His hatred for that man was incredible.* [**toward**]
   Tengo mucha admiración <u>por</u> ese autor. / *I have great admiration for that author.* [**toward**]
   Isabel tiene mucho amor <u>por</u> su esposo. / *Isabel has a lot of love for her husband.* [**toward**]

3. **Object of an errand after certain verbs of motion (ir** / *to go;* **enviar** / *to send;* **mandar** / *to send;* **venir** / *to come*). In this usage, it has the meaning of "*in search of.*"

   Fueron <u>por</u> pan. / *They went for bread.* [**in search of**]
   Me mandaron <u>por</u> el correo. / *They sent me for the mail.* [**in search of**]
   Viniste <u>por</u> el dinero que te debo. / *You came for the money that I owe you.* [**in search of**]

4. **Approximate location, space, or time.** Some of the English translations of this usage include: "*by,*" "*along,*" "*during,*" "*in,*" "*through.*"

   Ignacio viene <u>por</u> aquí / *Ignacio is coming this way.* [**by**]
   Él camina <u>por</u> la avenida. / *He is walking along the avenue.* [**along**]
   <u>Por</u> la mañana, no hay mucha gente. / *In the morning, there are not many people.* [**during, in**]
   Fuimos <u>por</u> Madrid. / *We went through Madrid.* [**through**]

5. **Duration of an action or time.** Some of the English translations of this usage include "*during,*" and "*throughout.*"

   Hablé <u>por</u> una hora. / *I spoke for an hour.* [**during**]
   Ella pagó <u>por</u> un año. / *She paid for a year.* [**during, throughout**]
   Vivimos en Santiago <u>por</u> dos años. / *We lived in Santiago for two years.* [**during**]

6. **Substitution and exchange.** Some of the English translations of this usage include: "*in exchange for,*" "*on behalf of,*" "*in place of.*"

   Cambié mis dólares estadounidenses <u>por</u> pesos mexicanos. / *I exchanged my U.S. dollars for Mexican pesos.* [***in exchange for***]
   Pagó diez pesos <u>por</u> el libro. / *He paid ten pesos for the book.* [**in exchange for**]
   Él me dio un libro <u>por</u> la revista. / *He gave me a book for the magazine.* [**in exchange for**]
   El decano habló <u>por</u> el jefe del departamento. / *The dean spoke for the department head.* [**on behalf of, in place of**].

7. **Multiplication, rate, and unit of measure.** Some of the English translations of this usage include: *"times," "X,"* and *"per."*

   Dos por dos son cuatro. / *Two times two is four.* [**times, X**]
   Recibe diez dólares por hora. / *He receives ten dollars per hour.* [**per**]
   No quiero pagar veinte por ciento. / *I don't want to pay twenty per cent.* [**per**]
   Quiero manejar a cien kilómetros por hora. / *I want to drive at 100 kilometers per hour.* [**per**]

8. **Means, manner, and agent.** The most common English translation of this usage is *"by."*

   Hablo muy poco por teléfono. / *I speak very little on the phone.* [**by, means**]
   Lo hicieron por fuerza. / *They did it by force.* [**by, manner**]
   La tarea fue hecha por Juan. / *The task was done by John.* [**by, agent**]

   The following are some common fixed expressions that indicate means and manner. They relate to transportation.

por autobús / *by bus*	**por coche** / *by car*
por avión / *by plane*	**por tren** / *by train*

   The following fixed expressions indicate means and manner and relate to communication.

por correo / *by mail*	**por teléfono** / *by telephone*
por correo electrónico / *by email*	

9. **Idiomatic or fixed expresssions.**

por ahora / *for the time being*	**por eso** / *therefore, for that reason*
por casualidad / *by accident*	**por gusto** / *for the fun of it*
por completo / *completely*	**por lo general** / *in general*
por consiguiente / *therefore*	**por lo tanto** / *therefore*
por Dios / *for God's sake*	**por lo visto** / *apparently*
por ejemplo / *for example*	**por otra parte** / *on the other hand*
por entonces / *at that time*	**por supuesto** / *of course*
por escrito / *in writing*	**por todas partes** / *everywhere*

10. **Idiomatic usage with estar** / *to be.* **Estar por** / *"to be about to."* Note that the infinitive of another verb always follows **estar por.**

    Estoy por partir. / *I'm about to leave.*
    Estoy por volver a casa ahora. / *I'm about to return.*
    Ella está por dormir ahora. / *She's about to sleep now.*

Exercise Set 2-2

A. Translate the following sentences.

1. Juan travels by train.

2. They (*m.*) went for pizza.

_____

3. She was about to cry.

_____

4. We travel by plane.

_____

5. You (*fam. sg.*) work hard for your family.

_____

6. Of course, I can go.

_____

7. I pay three dollars per liter.

_____

8. I am going to go for ice cream.

_____

9. The book was sold by the clerk (*m.*).

_____

10. He has much affection for his wife.

_____

11. I want the assignment in writing.

_____

12. Because of being sick, I did not work.

_____

B. Write as briefly as possible the reason for the use of **por** in each of the following sentences in the space provided. Refer to the previous discussion on the uses and meanings of **por**.

1. Estoy <u>por</u> visitar a Amparo. _____

2. La botella fue rota <u>por</u> Juan. _____

3. El coche fue alquilado <u>por</u> Enrique. _____

4. Pagué veinte dólares <u>por</u> ese libro. _____

5. Ella estudió <u>por</u> dos horas. _____

6. Ellos tienen compasión <u>por</u> él. _____

7. Cinco <u>por</u> cinco son veinticinco. _____

8. Ella maneja <u>por</u> la avenida principal. _____

9. Viajo <u>por</u> avión mucho. _____

10. Ella entra <u>por</u> la puerta anterior. _____

11. Muchas gracias <u>por</u> el regalo. _____

12. <u>Por</u> la tarde, tengo dos clases. _____

Exercise Set 2-3

In the following exercise, provide either **para** or **por**. Then give a reason for your choice based on the information provided in this chapter.

1. Estamos _____ (*about to*) ir a Chile.

   _____

2. Hornearé el pastel _____ el lunes.

   _____

3. _____ mí, no es posible.

   _____

4. Él tiene fuertes sentimientos _____ sus padres.

   _____

5. Cambio mi coche _____ uno nuevo.

   _____

6. La casa fue construida _____ esta compañía.

   _____

7. _____ ejemplo, no trabajo por la noche.

   _____

8. _____ recordar, escribo apuntes en mi cuaderno.

   _____

9. Él ruega mucho _____ ser religioso.

   _____

10. Trabajo _____ una fábrica.

    _____

11. Hay perros _____ todas partes.

    _____

12. _____ ir a Montevideo, pasamos _____ Buenos Aires.

    _____

Exercise Set 2-4

Write a complete sentence using the vocabulary below. Supply the correct form of **para** or **por** according to the context. On the second line, provide very briefly the reason for your choice of either **para** or **por**.

1. Marina/pasar/parque.   _____

   _____

2. Blas/hacer/esto/familia.   _____

   _____

3. Ernesto y Elena/hablarse/mucho/teléfono.   _____

   _____

4. Raquel/pagar/diez/euros/libro. _____

   _____

5. Eusebio/usar/tijeras/cortar/papel.   _____

   _____

Exercise Set 2-5

Complete the following sentences by filling in the blanks with the appropriate form of **para** or **por**.

1. El regalo es _____ Nicolás

2. Monterrat estudia _____ abogada.

3. Pablo viaja _____ Valencia.

4. Belén y Cristina van a llegar _____ la mañana.

5. ¿ _____quién es este libro?

6. Eva está _____ ir a Lima mañana.

7. Luis debe acostarse temprano _____ despertarse temprano.

8. Pilar viaja _____ avión.

9. Tomás recibe diez dólares _____ hora.

10. _____ el lunes próximo, deben leer toda la novela.

11. Pasamos _____ Madrid _____ llegar a Salamanca.

Para and *Por* in the Same Context

Thus far, we have looked at **para** and **por** in isolation with some exercises that involve making a distinction between these two prepositions. Students of Spanish often complain that when they say or write **para** or **por**, the instructor corrects them and tells them to use the other one.

There are situations in which either **para** or **por** may be used in the same context. You must remember, however, that there is <u>a change of meaning</u> when you use one or the other preposition. You need to remember, as we mentioned at the beginning of this chapter, that you must always think about what you mean. At first, this seems to be a laborious procedure, but, with time, it will become automatic, and you will be able to express yourself clearly.

In this final practice, we provide you with pairs of sentences that are identical except for the use of the prepositions **para** or **por**. We ask you to explain very briefly the semantic difference between the two sentences to help you to understand the different uses and meanings of these two prepositions.

Exercise Set 2-6

The following pairs of sentences are identical except for the presence of **para** or **por**. The use of either **para** or **por** changes the meaning of the sentence. In the space provided, explain the meaning of each sentence based on what you have learned in this lesson.

1. Vamos <u>para</u> Madrid. / Vamos <u>por</u> Madrid.

   _____

   _____

2. <u>Para</u> mí, no lo hizo mal. / <u>Por</u> mí, no lo hizo mal.

   _____

   _____

3. Vengo <u>para</u> trabajar. / Vengo <u>por</u> trabajar.

   _____

   _____

USES AND FEATURES

The following two tables with examples are intended for reviewing the main uses of **para** and **por** in Spanish.

Uses of *Para*	
1. To express purpose, "*in order to,*" or suitability.	**Mis apuntes son para organizar este tema.** / *My notes are to organize this theme.*
	Eusebio quiere levantarse temprano para llegar a tiempo. / *Eusebio wants to get up early in order to arrive on time.*
	Un dormitorio es un lugar para dormir. / *A dormitory is a place to sleep.*
2. To express motion toward a destination or goal.	**Mi hermana sale para Nicaragua mañana.** / *My sister is leaving for Nicaragua tomorrow.*
	Daniel estudia para maestro. / *Daniel studies to be a teacher.*
3. To express time limit or a specific point in time.	**Para mañana, ¡lean el capítulo doce!** / *By tomorrow, read Chapter Twelve.*
4. To express a comparison.	**Para principiante, Miguel tiene mucho talento.** / *For a beginner, Michael has a great deal of talent.*
5. To express a personal opinion.	**Para mí, el examen es difícil.** / *In my opinion, the exam is hard.*

Uses of *Por*	
1. To express motivation.	**Alfredo no lo hizo por su cansancio.** / *Alfredo did not do it because of his fatigue.*
2. To express emotion.	**Antonio expresa mucho amor por su padre.** / *Antonio expresses a lot of love for his father.*
3. To express the object of an errand after certain verbs of motion.	**Vengo por el libro de mi compañero.** / *I am coming for my companion's book.*
4. To express approximate location, space, or time.	**Enrique caminaba por el parque.** / *Enrique was walking through the park.*
	Pilar pasa por los dos coches. / *Pilar passes through (between) the two cars.*
	Alvaro estudió por tres horas. / *Alvaro studied for three hours.*
5. To express duration of an action or time.	**Alvaro estudió por tres horas.** / *Alvaro studied for three hours.*
	Mi hija durmió por ocho horas. / *My daughter slept for eight hours.*
6. To express substitution or exchange.	**Eva cambió sus dólares por lempiras.** / *Eva exchanged her dollars for lempiras.*
	Di mis sellos por sus monedas. / *I gave my stamps in exchange for his coins.*
7. To express multiplication, rate, and unit of measure.	**Tres por tres son nueve.** / *Three times three is nine.*
	Él tiene cuatro clientes por día. / *He has four clients per day.*
	Vas a Europa muchas veces por año. / *You go to Europe many times per year.*
8. To express "about to" with **estar** / *to be* followed by a verb in the infinitive.	**Amalia está por salir.** / *Amalia is about to leave.*

3

Verbs and Adjectives with Characteristic Prepositions

VERBS WITH INHERENT PREPOSITIONS

In English, there are certain verbs whose meaning includes an explicit preposition. When you look these verbs up in a standard English dictionary, the preposition is considered to be a part of the verb. Thus, there are Spanish verbs that correspond to two words in English. In a Spanish dictionary, however, these verbs consist of only an infinitive (the **-r** form of the verb). The preposition is thus contained in the basic meaning of these verbs. For this reason, it is not necessary to add a preposition after these verbs. It is already contained in their meaning!

The following Spanish verbs have inherent prepositions. The preposition is contained in the meaning, so it is not necessary to include it as an extra word in Spanish. The corresponding English verb consists of a verb plus a preposition which we indicate by means of an underline and boldface type.

Busco mi llave. / *I am looking **for** my key.*
Pago el libro. / *I'm paying **for** the book.*
Miro la televisión. / *I'm looking **at** the TV.*
Apago las luces. / *I'm turning **off** the lights.*
Enciendo las luces. / *I'm turning **on** the lights.*
Escucho mi música favorita. / *I'm listening **to** my favorite music.*

Grammar Note

Remember that when a noun that refers to a person is the direct object of a verb in Spanish, it is necessary to use the personal **a**. This is a function word that conveys that information, namely, the following word or phrase is a direct object that refers to a person. The following examples illustrate this. The presence of **a** in the Spanish sentence should **not** be construed as a translation of the inherent preposition.

Busco a Rafael. / *I am looking for Rafael.*
Miro a Irene. / *I am looking at Irene.*

150

> **Escucho a mi niño.** / *I am listening to my child.*
>
> Compare this usage with direct objects that refer to things. There is *no* personal **a**.
>
> **Busco mi llave.** / *I am looking for my key.*
> **Miro la televisión.** / *I am looking at the TV*
> **Escucho la música.** / *I am listening to the music.*

Verbs with Inherent Prepositions

In the following list and all subsequent lists, we follow the common dictionary convention of listing stem changes in parentheses (**ie**, **ue**, **i**). In the English translation, we indicate the preposition associated with each verb in **boldface** type.

agradecer	*to be thankful **for***
apagar	*to turn **off***
arrancar	*to turn **on***
atravesar (ie)	*to go **across***
averiguar	*to find **out***
bajar	*to go **down***
botar	*to throw **out***
buscar	*to look **for***
caerse	*to fall **down***
colgar (ue)	*to hang **up***
conocer	*to be acquainted **with**; to know*
cortar	*to cut **off**; to cut*
criar	*to bring **up**; to raise*
destacar	*to stand **out***
encender (ie)	*to turn **on***
entregar	*to hand **over***
envolver (ue)	*to wrap **up***
escuchar	*to listen **to***
esperar	*to wait **for**; to hope*
huir	*to flee **from***
ignorar	*to be unaware **of***
indicar	*to point **out***
llevar	*to take **away***
lograr	*to succeed **in***
mirar	*to look **at***
pagar	*to pay **for***
pedir (i, i)	*to ask **for***
platicar	*to talk **over**; to chat*
poner	*to turn **on**; to put; to place*

quitarse	*to take **off***
recoger	*to pick **up***
rogar (**ue**)	*to ask **for**; to pray **for***
saber	*to know **how to**; to know*
sacar	*to take **out***
subir	*to go **up***
yacer	*to lie **down***

Exercise Set 3-1

Translate the following sentences.

1. I ask for the bill.

   _____

2. They (*m.*) take out the garbage.

   _____

3. We point out the store.

   _____

4. You (*fam. sg.*) pay for the books with a check.

   _____

5. They (*m.*) listen to popular music.

   _____

6. She turns on the lights at night.

   _____

7. I thank her for the gifts.

   _____

8. He is looking for a novel.

   _____

9. I am waiting for my girlfriend.

   _____

10. I always look at the television.

    _____

11. I bring up my children.

    _____

12. They (*m.*) turn off the lights.

    _____

13. I take off my clothes.

_____

14. I go up the stairs.

_____

15. I succeed in doing the assignment.

_____

16. I am waiting for the bus.

_____

CHARACTERISTIC PREPOSITIONS

Some common verbs in Spanish are followed by what is called a "characteristic" preposition. This means that you must place this "distinctive" preposition before a following verb or noun. The most common characteristic prepositions are **a**, **con**, **de**, **en**, and **por**. They appear after a verb when it is followed either by another verb in the infinitive form (the form of the verb ending in **-r**), or by a noun or noun phrase. Sometimes they correspond to prepositions that are used in English, but in some instances they do not.

You will note that there are some conventions for dictionary entries of verbs in Spanish. First, stem changes are indicated in parentheses (**ie**; **ue**; **i**). Next, characteristic prepositions are indicated in parentheses (**a, con, de, en, por**). Finally, when characteristic prepositions are used with a verb, there is an indication about whether or not they may be followed by a verb (*v.*), a noun (*n.*), or both (*n., v.*).

The following examples illustrate all of these possibilities: **ir (a)** (*v., n.*) / *to go (to)*, **soñar (ue), (con)** (*v., n.*) / *to dream (about)*, **aprovecharse (de)** (*v., n.*) / *to take advantage (of)*, **insistir (en)** (*v., n.*) / *to insist (on)*, **preocuparse (por)** (*v., n.*) / *to worry (about)*.

> **Voy <u>a</u> estudiar.** / *I'm going to study.*
> **Voy <u>a</u> la tienda.** / *I'm going to the store.*
>
> **Sueño <u>con</u> dormir.** / *I dream about sleeping.*
> **Sueño <u>con</u> Elena.** / *I dream about Elena.*
>
> **Me quejo <u>de</u> hacer el trabajo.** / *I complain about doing the work..*
> **Me quejo <u>de</u> la tarea.** / *I complain about the homework.*
>
> **Insisto <u>en</u> volver a casa.** / *I insist on returning home.*
> **Insisto <u>en</u> este restaurante.** / *I insist on this restaurant.*
>
> **Me preocupo <u>por</u> tomar el examen.** / *I worry about taking the exam.*
> **Me preocupo <u>por</u> el examen.** / *I worry about the exam.*

> ### Grammar Note
>
> Remember that when there are two verbs in a row, it is the first one that is conjugated and the second one is normally an infinitive (form of the verb ending in **-r**), as the examples below illustrate.
>
> **Quiero estudiar mucho.** / *I want to study a lot.*
> **Prefiero beber café.** / *I prefer to drink coffee.*
>
> When a verb has a characteristic preposition, it goes before the infinitive:
>
> **Empiezo a fregar los platos.** / *I begin to clean the plates.*
> **Sueño con recibir un regalo.** / *I dream about receiving a gift.*
> **Ceso de fumar.** / *I stop smoking.*
> **Pienso en hacer la tarea.** / *I think about doing the assignment.*
> **Lucho por sobrevivir.** / *I struggle to survive.*

Verbs with the Characteristic Preposition *A*

The following is a list of verbs followed by the characteristic preposition **a** / *to*. In this and the following sections, we employ the commonly used dictionary conventions of parentheses to indicate the following information about each verb, as applicable: (1) stem-change (**ie**, **ue**, **i**); (2) characteristic preposition (**a**); (3) verb (*v.*) or noun (*n.*) that follows the characteristic preposition associated with the verb.

acercarse (**a**) (*n.*)	*to approach*
acertar (**a**) (*v.*)	*to manage; to succeed*
acostumbrarse (**a**) (*v., n.*)	*to become accustomed to*
adaptarse (**a**) (*v., n.*)	*to adapt oneself to*
adelantarse (**a**) (*v., n.*)	*to step forward to*
animar (**a**) (*v.*)	*to encourage*
aprender (**a**) (*v.*)	*to learn to do something*
apresurarse (**a**) (*v., n.*)	*to hasten; to hurry*
arriesgarse (**a**) (*v.*)	*to risk*
asistir (**a**) (*n.*)	*to attend*
aspirar (**a**) (*v., n.*)	*to aspire to*
atreverse (**a**) (*v.*)	*to dare to*
ayudar (**a**) (*v.*)	*to help to*
comenzar (**ie**) (**a**) (*v.*)	*to begin to*
consagrarse (**a**) (*n.*)	*to devote oneself to*
contribuir (**a**) (*v., n.*)	*to contribute to*
convidar (**a**) (*v., n.*)	*to invite to*
correr (**a**) (*v., n.*)	*to run to*
decidirse (**a**) (*v.*)	*to decide to*
dirigirse (**a**) (*v., n.*)	*to go to; to address; to direct oneself to*
empezar (**ie**) (**a**) (*v., n.*)	*to begin*
enseñar (**a**) (*v.*)	*to teach; to show how to*
forzar (**ue**) (**a**) (*v.*)	*to force to*

incitar (**a**) (*v.*)	*to incite to*
inspirar (**a**) (*v.*)	*to inspire to*
ir (**a**) (*v., n.*)	*to go to*
limitarse (**a**) (*v.*)	*to limit oneself to*
llegar (**a**) (*v., n.*)	*to be going to; to arrive at*
meterse (**a**) (*v.*)	*to take it upon oneself to*
negarse (**ie**) (**a**) (*v.*)	*to refuse to*
obligar (**a**) (*v.*)	*to force to*
oler (**ue**) (**a**) (*n.*)	*to smell like*
oponerse (**a**) (*v., n.*)	*to oppose*
parecerse (**a**) (*n.*)	*to resemble*
ponerse (**a**) (*v.*)	*to begin to*
reducirse (**a**) (*v., n.*)	*to reduce oneself to*
resignarse (**a**) (*v., n.*)	*to resign oneself to*
saber (**a**) (*n.*)	*to taste like*
subir (**a**) (*n.*)	*to climb; to go up*
venir (**a**) (*v., n.*)	*to come to*
volver (**ue**) (**a**) (*v., n.*)	*to do again; to return to*

Exercise Set 3-2

Translate the following sentences. Use the verbs from the list of verbs with the characteristic preposition **a**.

1. I return to Chile.

_____

2. We go to Mexico.

_____

3. She is becoming accustomed to driving.

_____

4. He arrives home early.

_____

5. You (*pol. sg.*) refuse to listen.

_____

6. You (*fam. sg.*) run to the park.

_____

7. They (*m.*) are learning to speak Spanish.

_____

8. I climb up the mountain.

_____

9. I decide to read.

_____

10. It smells like flowers.

_____

11. She shows me how to write well.

_____

12. My sister resembles Madonna.

_____

13. I encourage Carmen to read more.

_____

14. They (*m.*) hasten to study the lesson.

_____

15. We inspire her to study more.

_____

16. They (*m.*) arrive in Montevideo.

_____

Verbs with the Characteristic Preposition *Con*

The following is a list of verbs followed by the characteristic preposition **con** / *with*. We employ the commonly used dictionary conventions of parentheses to indicate the following information about each verb, as applicable: (1) stem-change (**ie, ue, i**); (2) characteristic preposition (**con**); (3) verb (*v.*) or noun (*n.*) that follows the characteristic preposition associated with the verb.

acabar (**con**) (*n.*)	*to finish with; to get rid of*
amenazar (**con**) (*v., n.*)	*to threaten with*
asociarse (**con**) (*n.*)	*to associate with*
bastar (**con**) (*v., n.*)	*to be sufficient; to have enough of*
casarse (**con**) (*n.*)	*to marry*
comparar (**con**) (*n.*)	*to compare with*
conformarse (**con**) (*v., n.*)	*to conform to*
contar (**ue**) (**con**) (*n.*)	*to count on*
contentarse (**con**) (*v., n.*)	*to content oneself with*
cumplir (**con**) (*n.*)	*to comply with*
dar (**con**) (*n.*)	*to come upon*
divertirse (**ie, i**) (**con**) (*n.*)	*to enjoy oneself with*
encararse (**con**) (*n.*)	*to face*
encariñarse (**con**) (*n.*)	*to be fond of*
enojarse (**con**) (*n.*)	*to get angry with*

juntarse (**con**) (*n.*)	*to join with*
llenar (**con**) (*n.*)	*to fill with*
salir (**con**) (*n.*)	*to go out with*
soñar (**ue**) (**con**) (*v., n.*)	*to dream of/about*
topar (**con**) (*n.*)	*to run across*
tropezar (**ie**) (**con**) (*n.*)	*to bump into*

Exercise Set 3-3

Translate the following sentences. Use the verbs from the list of verbs with the characteristic preposition **con**.

1. I get angry with my friend (*m.*).

   _____

2. She dreams about Buenos Aires.

   _____

3. He goes out with Elena.

   _____

4. They (*m.*) associate with important people.

   _____

5. He bumps into the chair.

   _____

6. I am finished with this work.

   _____

7. He is getting married to her.

   _____

8. I enjoy myself with my friends.

   _____

9. They (*m.*) comply with the law.

   _____

10. I fill the glass with milk.

    _____

11. I associate with nice people.

    _____

12. I content myself with music.

    _____

13. I conform to the customs.

_____

14. I count on my friends.

_____

15. I face the enemy (*m.*).

_____

16. I come upon my parents.

_____

Verbs with the Characteristic Preposition *De*

The following is a list of verbs followed by the characteristic preposition **de** / *of.* We employ the commonly used dictionary conventions of parentheses to indicate the following information about each verb as applicable: (1) stem-change (**ie, ue, i**); (2) characteristic preposition (**de**); (3) verb (*v.*) or noun (*n.*) that follows the characteristic preposition associated with the verb.

abusar (**de**) (*n.*)	*to take advantage of*
acabar (**de**) (*v.*)	*to have just*
acordarse (**ue**) (**de**) (*v., n.*)	*to remember*
alegrarse (**de**) (*v., n.*)	*to be happy to*
alejarse (**de**) (*n.*)	*to get away from*
aprovecharse (**de**) (*v., n.*)	*to take advantage of*
arrepentirse (**ie, i**) (**de**) (*v., n.*)	*to repent*
asombrarse (**de**) (*n.*)	*to be astonished at*
avergonzarse (**de**) (*n.*)	*to be ashamed of*
burlarse (**de**) (*n.*)	*to make fun of*
cansarse (**de**) (*v., n.*)	*to get tired of*
carecer (**de**) (*n.*)	*to lack*
cesar (**de**) (*v.*)	*to stop*
cuidar (**de**) (*n.*)	*to care for*
deber (**de**) (*v.*)	*suppose; must*
dejar (**de**) (*v.*)	*to stop*
depender (**de**) (*v., n.*)	*to depend on*
despedirse (**de**) (*n.*)	*to say good-bye to*
encargarse (**de**) (*v., n.*)	*to take charge of*
extrañarse (**de**) (*v., n.*)	*to be surprised at*
gozar (**de**) (*n.*)	*to enjoy*
haber (**de**) (*v.*)	*to have to*
huir (**de**) (*n.*)	*to flee*
indignarse (**de**) (*n.*)	*to be indignant at*
jactarse (**de**) (*v., n.*)	*to boast; to brag*
librarse (**de**) (*n.*)	*to get rid of*
llenarse (**de**) (*n.*)	*to fill up with*

maravillarse (**de**) (*n.*)	*to marvel at*
marcharse (**de**) (*n.*)	*to leave*
morir (**ue, u**) (**de**) (*n.*)	*to die of*
ocuparse (**de**) (*v., n.*)	*to pay attention to*
ofenderse (**de**) (*n.*)	*to be offended at*
olvidarse (**de**) (*v., n.*)	*to forget*
parar (**de**) (*v.*)	*to cease; to stop*
pensar (**ie**) (**de**) (*n.*)	*to have an opinion about*
preciarse (**de**) (*n.*)	*to boast about*
prescindir (**de**) (*v., n.*)	*to do without; to neglect*
quejarse (**de**) (*v., n.*)	*to complain about*
salir (**de**) (*n.*)	*to leave*
servir (**i, i**) (**de**) (*n.*)	*to serve as*
sorprenderse (**de**) (*n.*)	*to be surprised at*
sospechar (**de**) (*n.*)	*to be suspicious of*
tratar (**de**) (*v.*)	*to try to*
tratarse (**de**) (*v., n.*)	*to be a question of*

Exercise Set 3-4

Translate the following sentences. Use the verbs from the list of verbs with the characteristic preposition **de**.

1. This letter serves as a reminder.

   _____

2. She leaves the library.

   _____

3. They (*m.*) complain about everything.

   _____

4. You (*fam. sg.*) try to read many books.

   _____

5. I am dying of hunger.

   _____

6. She is stopping smoking.

   _____

7. He remembers his name now.

   _____

8. I marvel at his wisdom.

   _____

9. The weather depends on the season.

_____

10. I forget to go home at times.

_____

11. They (*m.*) get rid of the garbage.

_____

12. She leaves the building.

_____

13. She repents of her sins.

_____

14. We are tired of studying prepositions.

_____

15. I want to stop smoking.

_____

16. It depends on the weather.

_____

Verbs with the Characteristic Preposition *En*

The following is a list of verbs followed by the characteristic preposition **en** / *in/on*. We employ the commonly used dictionary conventions of parentheses to indicate the following information about each verb as applicable: (1) stem-change (**ie, ue, i**); (2) characteristic preposition (**en**); (3) verb (*v.*) or noun (*n.*) that follows the characteristic preposition associated with the verb.

complacerse (**en**) (*v., n.*)	*to take pleasure in*
confiar (**en**) (*v., n.*)	*to trust, to confide in*
consentir (**i, i**) (**en**) (*v.*)	*to consent to*
convenir (**en**) (*v., n.*)	*to agree to*
empeñarse (**en**) (*v., n.*)	*to insist on; to persist in*
fijarse (**en**) (*n.*)	*to notice*
influir (**en**) (*n.*)	*to influence*
insistir (**en**) (*v., n.*)	*to insist on*
ocuparse (**en**) (*v., n.*)	*to be busy with something*
pensar (**ie**) (**en**) (*v., n.*)	*to think about*
perseverar (**en**) (*v., n.*)	*to persevere in*
persistir (**en**) (*v., n.*)	*to persist in*
quedar (**en**) (*v., n.*)	*to agree on*
reparar (**en**) (*n.*)	*to notice*
tardar (**en**) (*v., n.*)	*to delay in*

Exercise Set 3-5

Translate the following sentences. Use the verbs from the list of verbs with the characteristic preposition **en**.

1. She delays in doing the work.

_____

2. I persist in reading the newspaper.

_____

3. I confide in my wife.

_____

4. They (*m.*) insist on going to Barcelona.

_____

5. She notices the car.

_____

6. We think about going to the beach a lot.

_____

7. He is busy with work.

_____

8. They (*m.*) consent to go.

_____

9. He takes pleasure in reading.

_____

10. She persists in singing.

_____

11. I notice her.

_____

12. You (*pol. pl.*) think about working late.

_____

13. They (*m.*) are busy with their relatives.

_____

14. I insist on going.

_____

Verbs with the Characteristic Preposition *Por*

The following is a list of verbs followed by the characteristic preposition **por** / *for*. We employ the commonly used dictionary conventions of parentheses to indicate the following information about each verb as applicable: (1) stem-change (**ie, ue, i**); (2) characteristic preposition (**por**); (3) verb (*v.*) or noun (*n.*) that follows the characteristic preposition associated with the verb.

abogar (**por**) (*n.*)	*to plead on behalf of*
acabar (**por**) (*v.*)	*to end up*
afanarse (**por**) (*v.*)	*to strive to*
apurararse (**por**) (*v., n.*)	*to fret over*
cambiar (**por**) (*n.*)	*to exchange*
desvivirse (**por**) (*n.*)	*to be crazy about*
esforzarse(ue) (**por**) (*v., n.*)	*to strive for / to*
estar (**por**) (*v., n.*)	*to be in favor of*
impacientarse (**por**) (*v., n.*)	*to become impatient for*
llorar (**por**) (*v., n.*)	*to cry for/about*
luchar (**por**) (*v., n.*)	*to struggle for*
mandar (**por**) (*n.*)	*to send via*
ofenderse (**por**) (*v., n.*)	*to be offended by*
optar (**por**) (*v., n.*)	*to choose; to opt for*
preguntar (**por**) (*n.*)	*to inquire about*
preocuparse (**por**) (*v., n.*)	*to worry about*
terminar (**por**) (*v.*)	*to end by*
trabajar (**por**) (*v., n.*)	*to strive for; to work for*
votar (**por**) (*n.*)	*to vote for*

Exercise Set 3-6

Translate the following sentences. Use the verbs from the list of verbs with the characteristic preposition **por**.

1. I worry about the exam.

   _____

2. They (*m.*) opt for traveling to Honduras.

   _____

3. She ends up by walking home.

   _____

4. They (*m.*) work for peace.

   _____

5. He cries about everything.

   _____

6. I strive for my son's future.

_____

7. We become impatient about leaving on time.

_____

8. They (*m.*) strive to arrive on time.

_____

9. You (*fam. sg.*) inquire about the money.

_____

10. I exchange dollars for pesos.

_____

11. I plead for my client.

_____

12. We strive to study more.

_____

13. I send the package by mail.

_____

14. You (*pol. sg.*) work for your family.

_____

15. We are in favor of that improvement.

_____

16. They (*m.*) opt for less work.

_____

Note

The verb **acabar** / *to finish, to complete* has the special idiomatic meaning "*to have just …*" when used with the preposition **de** and an infinitive:

Acabo <u>de</u> estudiar. / *I have just studied.*

The verb **volver (ue) (a)** / *to return* has the special idiomatic meaning "*to … again*" when used with the preposition **a** and an infinitive:

Vuelvo <u>a</u> estudiar / *I study again.*

The verb **ir (a)** / *to go* has the special idiomatic meaning "*to be going to …*" when used with the preposition **a** and an infinitive:

Voy <u>a</u> estudiar. / *I am going to study.*

Exercise Set 3-7

A. Translate the following sentences.

1. Pilar has just read this book.

   _____

2. We are going to go to Montevideo.

   _____

3. She is going to read that chapter again.

   _____

B. Provide the appropriate preposition in the blanks provided. Select from the prepositions **a, con, de, en, por**. If no preposition is necessary, leave the space blank.

1. Juan va _____ casa.

2. Ellos luchan _____ su hija.

3. Insistimos _____ beber café.

4. Busco _____ la revista.

5. Jorge se casa _____ Ana.

6. Él se burla _____ ella.

7. Subo _____ la montaña mañana.

8. Él cuelga _____ el teléfono.

9. Los padres confían _____ su hijo.

10. Me enojo _____ mi vecino.

11. Gustavo se aburre _____ este libro.

12. Tardas _____ llegar a tiempo.

13. Ella se impacienta _____ su hermana.

14. Miro _____ el libro.

15. Me preocupo _____ todo.

16. Le agradezco _____ el regalo.

ADJECTIVES WITH CHARACTERISTIC PREPOSITIONS

Some common adjectives also have characteristic prepositions. In some cases, these adjectives are derived from verbs that use the same inherent prepositions. Here is a list of the most common ones. You will note that a few of these may be used with two different prepositions. In some instances, there is a difference in meaning if there is a different preposition. In these cases, we use separate entries. The common prepositions used with these adjectives are **a**, **con**, **de**, **en**, **para**.

acompañado (**de**) (*n.*)	*accompanied by*
conforme (**a**, **con**) (*n.*)	*in accordance with*
contento (**con**, **de**) (*v.*, *n.*)	*happy with/about*
cubierto (**de**) (*n.*)	*covered with*
difícil (**de**) (*v.*)	*difficult to*
dotado (**de**) (*n.*)	*endowed with*
fácil (**de**) (*v.*)	*easy to*
falto (**de**) (*n.*)	*lacking in*
impropio (**de**) (*n.*)	*unbecoming of*
impropio (**para**) (*v.*, *n.*)	*unsuitable for*
libre (**de**) (*n.*)	*free of/from*
lleno (**de**) (*n.*)	*full of*
precedido (**de**) (*n.*)	*preceded by*
pronto (**a**) (*v.*)	*prone to*
pronto (**para**) (*v.*)	*ready to*
propio (**de**) (*n.*)	*appropriate to; becoming to*
propio (**para**) (*v.*, *n.*)	*suitable to/for*
responsable (**de**) (*v.*, *n.*)	*responsible for*
seguido (**de**) (*n.*)	*followed by*
seguro (**de**) (*v.*, *n.*)	*sure of*
último (**en**) (*v.*)	*last to*

Exercise Set 3-8

Translate the following sentences.

1. Teresa is happy with her family.

   _____

2. This jacket is suitable for Juan.

   _____

3. Isabel is accompanied by her husband.

   _____

4. Jorge is always the last to go home.

   _____

5. The car is covered with mud.

_____

6. We are free of debt.

_____

7. I'm ready to leave.

_____

8. Miguel is difficult to find.

_____

9. It is easy to read.

_____

10. She is responsible for arriving on time.

_____

11. It is difficult to study here.

_____

12. Alicia is endowed with much talent.

_____

USES AND FEATURES

1. Certain verbs in Spanish have a preposition as a basic part of their meaning. For this reason, it is not necessary to include a preposition in these cases. The following verbs are among the most common verbs of this type: **buscar** / _to look for_; **escuchar** / _to listen to_; **esperar** / _to wait for_; **mirar** / _to look at_; **pagar** / _to pay for_; **pedir** / _to ask for_.

2. Many verbs in Spanish, however, have characteristic prepositions when they are followed by a verb or a noun, and this is indicated by a following _v._ or _n._ in parentheses. The most common characteristic prepositions are **a, con, de, en, por**. The following are examples of such verbs: **comenzar (ie) (a)** / _to begin_; **soñar (ue) (con)** / _to dream of_; **cansarse (de)** / _to get tired of_; **jactarse (de)** / _to boast_; **tardar (en)** / _to delay in_; **luchar (por)** / _to struggle for_.

3. There are certain adjectives that are followed by characteristic prepositions. The most common ones are **a, con, de, en, para**. The following are examples: **pronto (a)** / _prone to_; **contento (con, de)** / _happy with/about_; **lleno (de)** / _full of_; **pronto (para)** / _ready to_.

4. After a preposition, you always use an infinitive (form of the verb ending in **-r**).

Review of Section 2 (Prepositions)

(Chapters 1–3)

Review Exercise Set 1-1

A. Use <u>one</u> of the following prepositions in the following blanks according to the meaning: **a**, **al**, **con**, **de**, **en**. You may repeat their use.

1. Voy _____ parque _____ el centro.

2. _____ pensar un momento, fui _____ casa.

3. Voy _____ la tienda _____ ellos.

4. _____ casa, estudio mucho.

5. Soledad es _____ Guatemala.

6. _____ hacer la tarea, me quedé dormido.

7. Bogota está _____ Colombia.

8. El libro es _____ Manuel.

9. Voy _____ estudiar hoy.

10. Es el once _____ mayo.

B. Supply one of the following prepositions according to the context: **a la derecha de**, **a lo largo de**, **al sur de**, **antes de**, **contigo**, **en lugar de**, **entre**, **hacia**, **hasta**, **según**. You may only use each preposition once.

1. México está _____ de los Estados Unidos.

2. _____ las ocho, estoy en la oficina.

3. _____ tú y yo, no lo sé.

4. Ella siempre va _____ la playa.

5. Quiero ir _____ .

6. _____ la ruta, hay muchas piedras.

7. _____ mañana.

8. Ellos viven _____ la plaza.

9. _____ té, voy a beber café.

10. _____ yo, no es necesario.

Review Exercise Set 1-2
Use either **para** or **por** according to the context.

1. _____ cantar bien, debo practicar mucho.

2. Ella está (about to) _____ ir a Miami mañana.

3. _____ fin, tengo unas vacaciones.

4. Mi hermana estudia _____ abogada.

5. Ellos dan un paseo (through) _____ el parque.

6. Necesito una taza _____ café.

7. Voy a Santiago _____ tren.

8. Estoy (inclined to) _____ estudiar ahora.

Review Exercise Set 1-3
Supply one of the following prepositions as needed: **a**, **con**, **de**, **en**, **por**. If no preposition is necessary, leave the space blank.

1. Voy _____ casa.

2. Me enojo _____ Alberto.

3. Ella se alegra _____ las noticias.

4. Tardamos _____ llegar.

5. Lloro _____ Alicia.

6. No es fácil _____ elegir.

7. El vaso está lleno _____ leche.

8. Cuelgo _____ el teléfono.

Appendices

Regular Verb Conjugations

This appendix contains the complete conjugation of three regular verbs: **hablar** / *to speak*; **comer** / *to eat*; and **vivir** / *to live*.

hablar / *to speak*

Infinitive	hablar
Present Participle	hablando
Past Participle	hablado

Present Indicative	
hablo	hablamos
hablas	habláis
habla	hablan

Preterit	
hablé	hablamos
hablaste	hablasteis
habló	hablaron

Imperfect Indicative	
hablaba	hablábamos
hablabas	hablabais
hablaba	hablaban

Present Perfect Indicative	
he hablado	hemos hablado
has hablado	habéis hablado
ha hablado	han hablado

Pluperfect (Past Perfect) Indicative	
había hablado	habíamos hablado
habías hablado	habíais hablado
había hablado	habían hablado

Future	
hablaré	hablaremos
hablarás	hablaréis
hablará	hablarán

Future Perfect	
habré hablado	habremos hablado
habrás hablado	habréis hablado
habrá hablado	habrán hablado

Conditional	
hablaría	hablaríamos
hablarías	hablaríais
hablaría	hablarían

Conditional Perfect	
habría hablado	habríamos hablado
habrías hablado	habríais hablado
habría hablado	habrían hablado

Present Subjunctive	
hable	hablemos
hables	habléis
hable	hablen

Imperfect Subjunctive	
hablara	habláramos
hablaras	hablarais
hablara	hablaran

Present Perfect Subjunctive	
haya hablado	hayamos hablado
hayas hablado	hayáis hablado
haya hablado	hayan hablado

Pluperfect (Past Perfect) Subjunctive	
hubiera hablado	hubiéramos hablado
hubieras hablado	hubierais hablado
hubiera hablado	hubieran hablado

Familiar Command	
¡habla! / ¡no hables!	¡hablad! / ¡no habléis!

Polite Command	
¡hable! / ¡no hable!	¡hablen! / ¡no hablen!

comer / *to eat*

Infinitive	comer
Present Participle	comiendo
Past Participle	comido

Present Indicative	
como	comemos
comes	coméis
come	comen

Preterit	
comí	comimos
comiste	comisteis
comió	comieron

Imperfect Indicative	
comía	comíamos
comías	comíais
comía	comían

Present Perfect Indicative	
he comido	hemos comido
has comido	habéis comido
ha comido	han comido

Pluperfect (Past Perfect) Indicative	
había comido	habíamos comido
habías comido	habíais comido
había comido	habían comido

Future	
comeré	comeremos
comerás	comeréis
comerá	comerán

Future Perfect	
habré comido	habremos comido
habrás comido	habréis comido
habrá comido	habrán comido

Conditional	
comería	comeríamos
comerías	comeríais
comería	comerían

Conditional Perfect	
habría comido	habríamos comido
habrías comido	habríais comido
habría comido	habrían comido

Present Subjunctive	
coma	comamos
comas	comáis
coma	coman

Imperfect Subjunctive	
comiera	comiéramos
comieras	comierais
comiera	comieran

Present Perfect Subjunctive	
haya comido	hayamos comido
hayas comido	hayáis comido
haya comido	hayan comido

Pluperfect (Past Perfect) Subjunctive	
hubiera comido	hubiéramos comido
hubieras comido	hubierais comido
hubiera comido	hubieran comido

Familiar Command	
¡come! / ¡no comas!	¡comed! / ¡no comáis!

Polite Command	
¡coma! / ¡no coma!	¡coman! / ¡no coman!

vivir / *to live*

Infinitive	vivir
Present Participle	viviendo
Past Participle	vivido

Present Indicative	
vivo	vivimos
vives	vivís
vive	viven

Preterit	
viví	vivimos
viviste	vivisteis
vivió	vivieron

Imperfect Indicative	
vivía	vivíamos
vivías	vivíais
vivía	vivían

Present Perfect Indicative	
he vivido	hemos vivido
has vivido	habéis vivido
ha vivido	han vivido

Pluperfect (Past Perfect) Indicative	
había vivido	habíamos vivido
habías vivido	habíais vivido
había vivido	habían vivido

Future	
viviré	viviremos
vivirás	viviréis
vivirá	vivirán

Future Perfect	
habré vivido	habremos vivido
habrás vivido	habréis vivido
habrá vivido	habrán vivido

Conditional	
viviría	viviríamos
vivirías	viviríais
viviría	vivirían

Conditional Perfect	
habría vivido	habríamos vivido
habrías vivido	habríais vivido
habría vivido	habrían vivido

Present Subjunctive	
viva	vivamos
vivas	viváis
viva	vivan

Imperfect Subjunctive	
viviera	viviéramos
vivieras	vivierais
viviera	vivieran

Present Perfect Subjunctive	
haya vivido	hayamos vivido
hayas vivido	hayáis vivido
haya vivido	hayan vivido

Pluperfect (Past Perfect) Subjunctive	
hubiera vivido	hubiéramos vivido
hubieras vivido	hubierais vivido
hubiera vivido	hubieran vivido

Familiar Command	
¡vive! / ¡no vivas!	¡vivid! / ¡no viváis!

Polite Command	
¡viva! / ¡no viva!	¡vivan! / ¡no vivan!

Reflexive Verb Conjugation

This appendix contains the complete conjugation of the regular reflexive verb **lavarse** / *to wash oneself.*

lavarse / *to wash oneself*

Infinitive	lavarse
Present Participle	lavándose
Past Participle	lavado

Present Indicative	
me lavo	nos lavamos
te lavas	os laváis
se lava	se lavan

Preterit	
me lavé	nos lavamos
te lavaste	os lavasteis
se lavó	se lavaron

Imperfect Indicative	
me lavaba	nos lavábamos
te lavabas	os lavabais
se lavaba	se lavaban

Present Perfect Indicative	
me he lavado	nos hemos lavado
te has lavado	os habéis lavado
se ha lavado	se han lavado

Pluperfect (Past Perfect) Indicative	
me había lavado	nos habíamos lavado
te habías lavado	os habíais lavado
se había lavado	se habían lavado

Future	
me lavaré	nos lavaremos
te lavarás	os lavaréis
se lavará	se lavarán

Future Perfect	
me habré lavado	nos habremos lavado
te habrás lavado	os habréis lavado
se habrá lavado	se habrán lavado

Conditional	
me lavaría	nos lavaríamos
te lavarías	os lavaríais
se lavaría	se lavarían

Conditional Perfect	
me habría lavado	nos habríamos lavado
te habrías lavado	os habríais lavado
se habría lavado	se habrían lavado

Present Subjunctive	
me lave	nos lavemos
te laves	os lavéis
se lave	se laven

Imperfect Subjunctive	
me lavara	nos laváramos
te lavaras	os lavarais
se lavara	se lavaran

Present Perfect Subjunctive	
me haya lavado	nos hayamos lavado
te hayas lavado	os hayáis lavado
se haya lavado	se hayan lavado

Pluperfect (Past Perfect) Subjunctive	
me hubiera lavado	nos hubiéramos lavado
te hubieras lavado	os hubierais lavado
se hubiera lavado	se hubieran lavado

Familiar Command	
¡lávate! / ¡no te laves!	¡lavaos! / ¡no os lavéis!

Polite Command	
¡lávese! / ¡no se lave!	¡lávense! / ¡no se laven!

Conjugation of *Ser, Estar, Tener, Hacer, Haber*

This appendix contains the complete conjugation of five common irregular verbs: **ser** / *to be* and **estar** / *to be*, **tener** / *to have*, **hacer** / *to do/ to make*, and the auxiliary verb **haber** / *to have*.

ser / *to be*

Infinitive	ser
Present Participle	siendo
Past Participle	sido

Present Indicative	
soy	somos
eres	sois
es	son

Preterit	
fui	fuimos
fuiste	fuisteis
fue	fueron

Imperfect Indicative	
era	éramos
eras	erais
era	eran

Present Perfect Indicative	
he sido	hemos sido
has sido	habéis sido
ha sido	han sido

Pluperfect (Past Perfect) Indicative	
había sido	habíamos sido
habías sido	habíais sido
había sido	habían sido

Future	
seré	seremos
serás	seréis
será	serán

Future Perfect	
habré sido	habremos sido
habrás sido	habréis sido
habrá sido	habrán sido

Conditional	
sería	seríamos
serías	seríais
sería	serían

Conditional Perfect	
habría sido	habríamos sido
habrías sido	habríais sido
habría sido	habrían sido

Present Subjunctive	
sea	seamos
seas	seáis
sea	sean

Imperfect Subjunctive	
fuera	fuéramos
fueras	fuerais
fuera	fueran

Present Perfect Subjunctive	
haya sido	hayamos sido
hayas sido	hayáis sido
haya sido	hayan sido

Pluperfect (Past Perfect) Subjunctive	
hubiera sido	hubiéramos sido
hubieras sido	hubierais sido
hubiera sido	hubieran sido

Familiar Command	
¡sé! / ¡no seas!	¡sed! / ¡no seáis!

Polite Command	
¡sea! / ¡no sea!	¡sean! / ¡no sean!

estar / *to be*

Infinitive	estar
Present Participle	estando
Past Participle	estado

Present Indicative	
estoy	estamos
estás	estáis
está	están

Preterit	
estuve	estuvimos
estuviste	estuvisteis
estuvo	estuvieron

Imperfect Indicative	
estaba	estábamos
estabas	estabais
estaba	estaban

Present Perfect Indicative	
he estado	hemos estado
has estado	habéis estado
ha estado	han estado

Pluperfect (Past Perfect) Indicative	
había estado	habíamos estado
habías estado	habíais estado
había estado	habían estado

Future	
estaré	estaremos
estarás	estaréis
estará	estarán

Future Perfect	
habré estado	habremos estado
habrás estado	habréis estado
habrá estado	habrán estado

Conditional	
estaría	estaríamos
estarías	estaríais
estaría	estarían

Conditional Perfect	
habría estado	habríamos estado
habrías estado	habríais estado
habría estado	habrían estado

Present Subjunctive	
esté	estemos
estés	estéis
esté	estén

Imperfect Subjunctive	
estuviera	estuviéramos
estuvieras	estuvierais
estuviera	estuvieran

Present Perfect Subjunctive	
haya estado	hayamos estado
hayas estado	hayáis estado
haya estado	hayan estado

Pluperfect (Past Perfect) Subjunctive	
hubiera estado	hubiéramos estado
hubieras estado	hubierais estado
hubiera estado	hubieran estado

Familiar Command	
¡está! / ¡no estés!	¡estad! / ¡no estéis!

Polite Command	
¡esté! / ¡no esté!	¡estén! / ¡no estén!

tener / *to have*

Infinitive	tener
Present Participle	teniendo
Past Participle	tenido

Present Indicative	
tengo	tenemos
tienes	tenéis
tiene	tienen

Preterit	
tuve	tuvimos
tuviste	tuvisteis
tuvo	tuvieron

Imperfect Indicative	
tenía	teníamos
tenías	teníais
tenía	tenían

Present Perfect Indicative	
he tenido	hemos tenido
has tenido	habéis tenido
ha tenido	han tenido

Pluperfect (Past Perfect) Indicative	
había tenido	habíamos tenido
habías tenido	habíais tenido
había tenido	habían tenido

Future	
tendré	tendremos
tendrás	tendréis
tendrá	tendrán

Future Perfect	
habré tenido	habremos tenido
habrás tenido	habréis tenido
habrá tenido	habrán tenido

Conditional	
tendría	tendríamos
tendrías	tendríais
tendría	tendrían

Conditional Perfect	
habría tenido	habríamos tenido
habrías tenido	habríais tenido
habría tenido	habrían tenido

Present Subjunctive	
tenga	tengamos
tengas	tengáis
tenga	tengan

Imperfect Subjunctive	
tuviera	tuviéramos
tuvieras	tuvierais
tuviera	tuvieran

Present Perfect Subjunctive	
haya tenido	hayamos tenido
hayas tenido	hayáis tenido
haya tenido	hayan tenido

Pluperfect (Past Perfect) Subjunctive	
hubiera tenido	hubiéramos tenido
hubieras tenido	hubierais tenido
hubiera tenido	hubieran tenido

Familiar Command	
¡ten! / ¡no tengas!	¡tened! / ¡no tengáis!

Polite Command	
¡tenga! / ¡no tenga!	¡tengan! / ¡no tengan!

hacer / *to do* / *to make*

Infinitive	hacer
Present Participle	haciendo
Past Participle	hecho

Present Indicative	
hago	hacemos
haces	hacéis
hace	hacen

Preterit	
hice	hicimos
hiciste	hicisteis
hizo	hicieron

Imperfect Indicative	
hacía	hacíamos
hacías	hacíais
hacía	hacían

Present Perfect Indicative	
he hecho	hemos hecho
has hecho	habéis hecho
ha hecho	han hecho

Pluperfect (Past Perfect) Indicative	
había hecho	habíamos hecho
habías hecho	habíais hecho
había hecho	habían hecho

Future	
haré	haremos
harás	haréis
hará	harán

Future Perfect	
habré hecho	habremos hecho
habrás hecho	habréis hecho
habrá hecho	habrán hecho

Conditional	
haría	haríamos
harías	haríais
haría	harían

Conditional Perfect	
habría hecho	habríamos hecho
habrías hecho	habríais hecho
habría hecho	habrían hecho

Present Subjunctive	
haga	hagamos
hagas	hagáis
haga	hagan

Imperfect Subjunctive	
hiciera	hiciéramos
hicieras	hicierais
hiciera	hicieran

Present Perfect Subjunctive	
haya hecho	hayamos hecho
hayas hecho	hayáis hecho
haya hecho	hayan hecho

Pluperfect (Past Perfect) Subjunctive	
hubiera hecho	hubiéramos hecho
hubieras hecho	hubierais hecho
hubiera hecho	hubieran hecho

Familiar Command	
¡haz! / ¡no hagas!	¡haced! / ¡no hagáis!

Polite Command	
¡haga! / ¡no haga!	¡hagan! / ¡no hagan!

haber / *to have* (Auxiliary)

Infinitive	haber
Present Participle	habiendo
Past Participle	habido

Present Indicative	
he	hemos
has	habéis
ha	han

Preterit	
hube	hubimos
hubiste	hubisteis
hubo	hubieron

Imperfect Indicative	
había	habíamos
habías	habíais
había	habían

Present Perfect Indicative	
he habido	hemos habido
has habido	habéis habido
ha habido	han habido

Pluperfect (Past Perfect) Indicative	
había habido	habíamos habido
habías habido	habíais habido
había habido	habían habido

Future	
habré	habremos
habrás	habréis
habrá	habrán

Future Perfect	
habré habido	habremos habido
habrás habido	habréis habido
habrá habido	habrán habido

Conditional	
habría	habríamos
habrías	habríais
habría	habrían

Conditional Perfect	
habría habido	habríamos habido
habrías habido	habríais habido
habría habido	habrían habido

Present Subjunctive	
haya	hayamos
hayas	hayáis
haya	hayan

Imperfect Subjunctive	
hubiera	hubiéramos
hubieras	hubierais
hubiera	hubieran

Present Perfect Subjunctive	
haya habido	hayamos habido
hayas habido	hayáis habido
haya habido	hayan habido

Pluperfect (Past Perfect) Subjunctive	
hubiera habido	hubiéramos habido
hubieras habido	hubierais habido
hubiera habido	hubieran habido

Familiar Command	
¡hé! / ¡no hayas!	¡habed! /¡no hayáis!

Polite Command	
¡haya! / ¡no haya!	¡hayan! / ¡no hayan!

Answers to Section 1 (Pronouns)

CHAPTER 1

Exercise Set 1-1

1. tú
2. usted
3. ustedes
4. vosotras
5. ustedes

Exercise Set 1-2

1. Es probable.
2. Es de María.
3. Llueve.
4. Son las ocho de la noche.
5. Es temprano.
6. Es de metal.
7. Es nuevo.
8. Es la medianoche.
9. Está aquí.
10. Es un coche.

Exercise Set 1-3

1. hablo
2. caminamos
3. cantan
4. estudias
5. baila
6. tocáis

Exercise Set 1-4

1. comes
2. bebéis
3. corremos
4. leen
5. vendo
6. rompe

Exercise Set 1-5

1. vives
2. abrimos

3. escribe
4. cubrís
5. sufren
6. admito

Exercise Set 1-6

A.

1. nosotros, nosotras
2. yo
3. vosotros, vosotras
4. él, ella, Ud.
5. ellos, ellas, Uds.
6. él, ella, Ud.
7. nosotros, nosotras
8. tú
9. ellos, ellas, Uds.
10. él, ella, Ud.
11. nosotros, nosotras
12. vosotros, vosotras
13. él, ella, Ud.
14. yo

B.

1. Ud.
2. tú
3. Uds.
4. Uds.
5. Uds.
6. vosotros
7. Ud.
8. Uds.

Exercise Set 1-7

1. Jorge, tú comes aquí.
2. Marta y Elena, vosotras escribís la carta.
3. Señores Rodríguez, Uds. cantan bien.
4. Profesor(a) Smith, Ud. habla español muy bien.
5. Juan y yo trabajamos mucho.
6. Es tarde.
7. Es la una.
8. Son las dos.

9. Nosotros/-as hablamos español.
10. Ella vive aquí.

CHAPTER 2

Exercise Set 2-1

1. ¿Quién es ella?
2. ¿Quiénes son los hombres?
3. ¿Quién es él?
4. ¿Quiénes son Uds.?

Exercise Set 2-2

1. ¿A quién llamas?
2. ¿A quiénes conoces?
3. ¿A quiénes quieres ver?
4. ¿A quién necesitas?

Exercise Set 2-3

1. ¿De quién es el libro?
2. ¿De quiénes es la casa?
3. ¿De quién es el café?
4. ¿De quiénes son las cartas?

Exercise Set 2-4

1. ¿Quiénes son ellos?
2. ¿De quién es el bolígrafo?
3. ¿A quién busca Ud.?
4. ¿Quién es la mujer?
5. ¿A quiénes quieres ver?
6. ¿De quiénes es el coche?
7. ¿Quién es?
8. ¿A quiénes conoces?
9. ¿De quién es el libro?
10. ¿Quién está aquí?
11. ¿Quién bebe café?
12. ¿De quién es el gato?
13. ¿A quiénes llamas?
14. ¿Quién tiene el coche?

Exercise Set 2-5

1. ¿Cuál? ¿Cuál es tu nombre?
2. ¿Qué? ¿Qué es?
3. ¿Qué? ¿Qué color quieres?
4. ¿Qué? ¿Qué estudiante está aquí?
5. ¿Qué? ¿Qué haces?
6. ¿Cuáles? ¿Cuáles necesitas?
7. ¿Cuál? ¿Cuál de los dos quieres?
8. ¿Qué? ¿Qué palabras recuerdas?
9. ¿Qué? ¿Qué día es hoy?
10. ¿Cuál? ¿Cuál es tu dirección?

Exercise Set 2-6

1. ¿De quién es el dinero?
2. ¿Quién es él?
3. ¿Cuál es la capital de España?
4. ¿A quién miras?
5. ¿Qué es?
6. ¿De quiénes son las cartas?
7. ¿A quiénes ve ella?
8. ¿Cuáles son las partes de una computadora?
9. ¿Quiénes son tus amigos?

CHAPTER 3

Exercise Set 3-1

1. El libro está cerca de ella.
2. Ella está delante de mí.
3. El coche es para ti.
4. El libro está al lado de Ud.
5. El regalo es para vosotros.
6. Ellos viven a la derecha de nosotros.
7. El libro es de ella.
8. Él está con Uds.
9. Ella está a la izquierda de ti.
10. Ellos están delante de ella.

Exercise Set 3-2

1. excepto (salvo, menos) yo
2. excepto (salvo, menos) tú
3. según yo
4. entre tú y yo

Exercise Set 3-3

1. Tengo un libro para ti.
2. Ellos están delante de mí.
3. Estamos al lado de ellas.
4. Ellos viven cerca de Uds.
5. El regalo es de él.
6. La librería está enfrente de nosotros.
7. Según yo, ella está aquí.
8. Entre tu y yo, es posible.
9. Es para vosotras.
10. No recuerdo y no quiero hablar de ello.
11. Todos, menos (excepto, salvo) yo, comen pizza.
12. Como con Uds.
13. Vivo cerca de ella.
14. Ellos están delante de ti.

Exercise Set 3-4

1. Él trae el coche consigo.
2. Ella viene conmigo.
3. Bailo con ella.
4. Ellos van contigo.
5. Comemos con ellos.
6. Ella vive con él.
7. Ellos traen la comida consigo.
8. Ellos hablan con Ud.

Exercise Set 3-5

1. Ella va conmigo.
2. Según él, llueve.
3. Para ellos, María canta bien.
4. Él siempre trae su libro consigo.
5. Ellos están cerca de mí.
6. Él estudia con ella.
7. Son para ti.
8. Incluso yo, hay tres estudiantes.
9. Ellos están contigo.
10. Ellos viven al lado de nosotros.

CHAPTER 4

Exercise Set 4-1

1. Mario los compra.
2. Rosa y Claudio lo venden.
3. La compramos aquí.
4. Ellos lo beben.
5. Ella lo estudia.
6. Ellos la ven.
7. Los necesito.
8. Los vemos.
9. La canto.
10. Lo temo.

Exercise Set 4-2

A.
1. Aurelio las lee.
2. Esperanza está bebiéndolo. Esperanza lo está bebiendo.
3. Quieres cantarla. La quieres cantar.
4. La escribo.
5. Ella los come.

B.
1. La veo aquí.
2. Necesitas mirarla. La necesitas mirar.
3. Ella está leyéndolo ahora. Ella lo está leyendo ahora.

4. Ellos no lo necesitan.
5. Él nos ve.
6. Los tenemos.
7. Ellos no necesitan escribirla. Ellos no la necesitan escribir.
8. No estoy comiéndola. No la estoy comiendo.
9. La vemos a Ud.
10. Ellos quieren llamarla. Ellos la quieren llamar.

C.
1. Los leo.
2. Quiero hacerlo. Lo quiero hacer.
3. Estamos leyéndolo. Lo estamos leyendo.

D.
1. Raúl no lo bebe.
2. Salvador y Gloria no quieren estudiarla. Salvador y Gloria no la quieren estudiar.
3. No estoy leyéndola. No la estoy leyendo.
4. No la escribimos.
5. Camilo no necesita hacerlo. Camilo no lo necesita hacer.

CHAPTER 5

Exercise Set 5-1

1. Le hablo a ella en español.
2. Les damos el localizador a ellos.
3. Ellos van a vendernos el teléfono celular. Ellos nos van a vender el teléfono celular.
4. Él está mandándonos el correo electrónico. Él nos está mandando el correo electrónico.

Exercise Set 5-2

1. No le doy el control remoto a él.
2. Ellos no nos hablan en inglés.
3. Ellos no deben mostrarles el videojuego a ellos. Ellos no les deben mostrar el videojuego a ellos.
4. Ud. no está mandándole el organizador a él. Ud. no le está mandando el organizador a él.

Exercise Set 5-3

A.
1. Le digo la verdad a ella.
2. Ellos necesitan escribirles la carta a ellos. Ellos les necesitan escribir la carta a ellos.

3. Ellos están hablándonos en español. Ellos nos están hablando en español.
4. Él debe hablarme. Él me debe hablar.
5. Ellos no le venden el coche a ella.
6. Ella me muestra la casa.
7. Ellos les hablan a Uds.
8. No voy a darle el dinero a él. No le voy a dar el dinero a él.

B.

1. Le doy los libros a ella.
2. Prefiero darle los regalos a ella. Le prefiero dar los regalos a ella.
3. Estoy entregándole el paquete a él. Le estoy entregando el paquete a él.
4. Te vendo el coche.
5. Les hablo a Uds. en español.

Exercise Set 5-4

1. "The books are pleasing to me." Me gustan los libros.
2. "The restaurant is pleasing to my friends." A mis amigos les gusta el restaurante.
3. "Watching soap operas is pleasing to you." Te gusta mirar las telenovelas.
4. "The car is pleasing to her." A ella le gusta el coche.
5. "The magazines are pleasing to them." A ellos les gustan las revistas.
6. "Is the food pleasing to you?" ¿A usted le gusta la comida?
7. "You are pleasing to me." Me gustas.
8. "You fall well to me." Me caes bien.
9. "Swimming in the sea is pleasing to you." A ustedes les gusta nadar en el mar.
10. "To sing is pleasing to us." Nos gusta cantar.

Exercise Set 5-5

1. "The books are not pleasing to me." No me gustan los libros.
2. "The headphones are not pleasing to us." No nos gustan los auriculares.
3. "The battery charger is not pleasing to you." No te gusta el cargador de pilas.
4. "The program is not pleasing to him." A él no le gusta el programa.
5. "The CD is not pleasing to them." A ellos no les gusta el disco compacto.

Exercise Set 5-6

A.

1. "The tooth is aching to her." A ella le duele el diente.
2. "Twenty euros are lacking to me." Me faltan veinte euros.
3. "The books are not interesting to me." No me interesan los libros.
4. "Foolish people are a bother to him." A él le molesta la gente tonta.
5. "To work suits your interest." Te conviene trabajar.

B.

1. ¿A Ud. le gusta la literatura?
2. ¿A Uds. les gustan los museos?
3. ¿A Ud. le interesa ir al teatro?
4. ¿A Uds. les falta el dinero?
5. ¿A Ud. le bastan cien pesos?
6. ¿A Ud. le importa leer la revista?
7. ¿A Ud. le encanta la película?

CHAPTER 6

Exercise Set 6-1

A.

1. Nicolás se las escribe a ellos.
2. Amparo está contándoselo a él. Amparo se lo está contando.
3. Fidel necesita vendérsela a ella. Fidel se la necesita vender a ella.
4. Ellas están dándoselo a ellos. Ellas se lo están dando a ellos.
5. Guillermo me la muestra.

B.

1. Ellos nos los venden.
2. Queremos mostrárselas a ellos. Se las queremos mostrar a ellos.
3. Él está dándoselo a ella. Él se lo está dando a ella.

C.

1. Se las muestro a ella.
2. Voy a escribírsela a ellos. Se la voy a escribir a ellos.
3. Estoy dándoselo a él. Se lo estoy dando a él.

D.

1. No se la canto a Berta.
2. No se la digo a mis amigos.
3. No quiero hablárselo a mi familia.
4. No se lo voy a regalar a mis niños.

5. No estoy haciéndoselo a mi esposa.
6. No se lo estoy dando a ella.

Exercise Set 6-2

1. se los
2. se lo
3. selos
4. sela
5. Se la

CHAPTER 7

Exercise Set 7-1

A.

1. Las mujeres se despiertan, se levantan, se duchan y se visten.
2. Me acuerdo de la fecha de hoy.
3. Él se mira en el espejo siempre.
4. Ellos se acuestan a las once.
5. Cuando trabajamos tarde, nos cansamos.
6. Ella se preocupa mucho por los exámenes.
7. Si no comes bien, te enfermas.
8. Él se enoja cuando él se levanta temprano.
9. Nos dormimos por la tarde después del almuerzo.
10. Cuando ellos se sientan, ellos miran la televisión.
11. Me lavo el pelo.

B.

1. Voy a casarme. Me voy a casar.
2. Ella quiere sentarse. Ella se quiere sentar.
3. Ellos necesitan levantarse. Ellos se necesitan levantar.

C.

1. Estamos cansándonos. Nos estamos cansando.
2. Estoy enojándome. Me estoy enojando.

D.

1. Lavo a mi hijo.
2. Ellos despiertan a sus niños.
3. Llamamos a nuestros padres.
4. Ella viste a su hija.
5. Ellos acuestan a sus hijos.

Exercise Set 7-2

1. Nos abrazamos.
2. Ellos se conocen bien.
3. Ustedes se ven.
4. Ellas se escriben.
5. Nos gritamos a veces.

6. Vosotros os veis.
7. Los amigos se compran regalos.
8. Ellos se dicen secretos.
9. Nos mandamos cartas.
10. Ellos se hablan por teléfono cada día.

Exercise Set 7-3

1. Te hablas a ti mismo.
2. Nos hablamos a nosotros mismos.
3. Me lavo a mí mismo.

Exercise Set 7-4

1. Los primos se abrazan el uno al otro. Los primos se abrazan unos a otros.
2. Nos vemos a nosotros mismos.
3. Los recién casados se besan el uno a la otra frecuentemente.
4. Ellos se gritan el uno al otro (mutuamente).
5. Ellos se miran el uno al otro (mutuamente).

CHAPTER 8

Exercise Set 8-1

1. Se pagan las cuentas los lunes.
2. Se habla español aquí.
3. Se necesita una secretaria bilingüe.
4. Se reparan computadoras aquí.
5. Se venden tacos en este restaurante.
6. Se venden carne y pescado aquí.
7. Se invita a los amigos.
8. Se producen coches en Detroit.
9. Se cierran los museos los lunes en España.
10. Se vende ropa en esta tienda.
11. Se toca música popular aquí.
12. Se invitó a los parientes.
13. Se eligió al presidente hoy.
14. Se publica el periódico cada semana.

Exercise Set 8-2

1. Se venden periódicos aquí.
2. Se deben comer tres comidas cada día.
3. No se debe fumar.
4. Se baila el flamenco aquí.
5. No se pueden sacar fotos aquí.
6. Se debe hacer ejercicio cada día.
7. Se puede nadar en esta playa.
8. Se debe estudiar cada día.
9. ¿Se puede entrar aquí?
10. Se dice que hace calor hoy.

CHAPTER 9

Exercise Set 9-1

1. Tengo mi coche y ella tiene el suyo. Tengo mi coche y ella tiene el de ella.
2. Compramos nuestra comida aquí y tú compras la tuya aquí también.
3. Ella tiene un gato negro y el mío es amarillo.
4. Mis libros están en casa y los suyos están en la oficina. Mis libros están en casa y los de él están en la oficina.
5. Haces tu tarea y ella hace la suya. Haces tu tarea y ella hace la de ella.
6. Mi oficina está cerca y la suya está lejos. Mi oficina está cerca y la de ellos está lejos.
7. Nuestro apartamento está en las afueras y el de Ud. está en la ciudad.
8. Mi novia es rubia y la suya es morena. Mi novia es rubia y la de él es morena.

Exercise Set 9-2

A.

1. La computadora es mía.
2. Las computadoras son mías.
3. La revista es nuestra.
4. Las revistas son nuestras.
5. El coche es suyo. El coche es de él.
6. Los coches son suyos. Los coches son de él.
7. El perro es tuyo.
8. Los perros son tuyos.
9. El periódico es suyo. El periódico es de ellos.
10. Los periódicos son suyos. Los periódicos son de ellos.
11. La camisa es suya. La camisa es de Ud.
12. Las camisas son suyas. Las camisas son de Ud.

B.

1. Es mío.
2. Es suya. Es de ellos.
3. Son nuestras.
4. Es tuya
5. Es vuestro.
6. Es suyo. Es de ellos.
7. Son suyos. Son de él.
8. Es mío.
9. Son suyos. Son de Uds.
10. Es nuestra.

CHAPTER 10

Exercise Set 10-1

1. Esta casa es vieja, pero ésa es nueva.
2. Aquel coche es rojo, pero éste es azul.
3. Estas novelas son interesantes, pero ésas son terribles.
4. Aquellos niños están contentos, pero éstos están tristes.
5. Este libro es mío, pero aquél es de Eva.
6. Me gusta ese color, pero éste no.
7. Tengo esta película, pero aquélla no.
8. Estos vecinos son simpáticos, pero ésos son antipáticos.

Exercise Set 10-2

1. ¡Eso es estúpido!
2. Esto es mi error.
3. Aquello es un problema.

Exercise Set 10-3

1. Tengo dos hijas y dos hijos. Aquéllas son morenas y ésos son rubios.

CHAPTER 11

Exercise Set 11-1

A.

1. los azules
2. la grande
3. las populares
4. la mexicana
5. el viejo
6. las bonitas
7. el interesante
8. los mexicanos
9. la sabrosa
10. los domésticos
11. el rojo

B.

1. Como las comidas grandes y ella come las pequeñas.
2. El coche negro es mío y el gris es tuyo.
3. La mujer rubia es mi hermana y la pelirroja es mi prima.
4. Tengo un coche azul y mi esposa tiene uno amarillo.
5. Tengo juguetes viejos, pero los nuevos son de mi hijo.

Exercise Set 11-2

1. lo viejo y lo nuevo
2. lo útil
3. lo mío
4. lo actual
5. lo pasado

Exercise Set 11-3

1. El primer examen es más difícil que el segundo.
2. Mi casa es la cuarta a la derecha y mis amigos viven en la quinta.
3. El primer mes es enero. El séptimo es julio, y el noveno es septiembre.
4. La segunda novela es mejor que la primera.
5. La octava sinfonía es mejor que la cuarta.

Exercise Set 11-4

1. Mi amigo tiene pocos libros, pero yo tengo trescientos.
2. Enrique tiene dos coches, y yo tengo uno.
3. Tengo una computadora, pero necesito dos.
4. La familia de Elena tiene cuatro teléfonos celulares, pero nosotros tenemos sólo uno.
5. Tengo un gato, pero Carmen tiene tres.

Exercise Set 11-5

1. Tengo demasiado.
2. Ella necesita uno.
3. Pocas están abiertas ahora.
4. María bebe mucha.
5. Ellos ofrecen varios.
6. Vendemos ambas.
7. Tengo algunas aquí.
8. Él quiere varias.
9. Tenemos otra.
10. Otros van a la biblioteca.

Exercise Set 11-6

1. ¿Viene alguien?
2. No viene nadie. Nadie viene.
3. ¿Tienes algo?
4. No tengo nada.
5. ¿Necesitas algunas recetas?
6. No tengo ninguna.

CHAPTER 12

Exercise Set 12-1

1. Ella tiene los boletos que quiero.
2. Veo al hombre que va a la tienda.

3. El regalo, que es muy caro, está en el coche.
4. Ésta es la mujer que quiere ir a la oficina.
5. Hay muchos estudiantes que quieren ir a la biblioteca.
6. Tengo el reporte que buscas.
7. La mujer que está en la oficina es mi prima.
8. La computadora que me gusta está aquí.
9. Camino por el parque que está en el centro.
10. Veo a la mujer que enseña a mi clase.

Exercise Set 12-2

1. Berta, quien es de Guatemala, está aquí.
2. Mis parientes, quienes viven en Chicago, hablan muchas lenguas.
3. Alicia, al lado de quien estás sentado, es famosa.
4. Juan, a quien conoces, es estudiante en la universidad.
5. Mi novia, quien es de Madrid, vive aquí ahora.
6. Los amigos, a quienes invitamos, están atrasados.
7. La mujer con quien bailas es Graciela.
8. Federico es la persona para quien ella hace muchos sacrificios.
9. La muchacha, quien come mucho helado, tiene un hermano.
10. El médico a quien conocemos es muy bueno.

Exercise Set 12-3

1. La novela, la cual (la que, que) leo, es de Gabriel García Márquez.
2. Esta cerveza, la cual (la que, que) me gusta mucho, es mexicana.
3. La calle en la cual (al que, que) vivo no tiene tráfico.
4. Ésta es la película en la cual (la que, que) el actor gana un premio.
5. El que estudia mucho, aprende mucho.
6. Los que viajan mucho están a menudo cansados.

Exercise Set 12-4

1. Esta mujer, cuyo perro es pequeño, tiene un marido simpático.
2. Ese hombre, cuya hija está casada, tiene una nieta.
3. María, cuyos amigos trabajan en la ciudad, tiene un trabajo en los suburbios.

4. Esa biblioteca, cuyas puertas siempre están abiertas, tiene muchos libros.
5. Estas casas, cuyas ventanas están rotas, son viejas.

Exercise Set 12-5

1. Lo que es interesante es lo que ella dice.
2. Estudio español mucho, lo cual es importante.

Exercise Set 12-6

1. a quien
2. Lo que
3. que
4. con quien
5. cuyo
6. la cual
7. los cuales
8. el cual

ANSWERS TO REVIEW OF SECTION 1 (PRONOUNS)

Review Exercise Set 1-1

A.

1. tú
2. Uds.
3. vosotros
4. Uds.
5. Uds.

B.

1. habla
2. bebemos
3. escriben
4. compras
5. vivís
6. canta
7. leo
8. estudia

C.

1. Es posible.
2. Es tarde.
3. Está aquí.
4. Llueve.
5. Es un libro.

Review Exercise Set 1-2

1. ¿Cuál?
2. ¿Quiénes?
3. ¿Quién?
4. ¿Qué?
5. ¿Cuáles?

Review Exercise Set 1-3

1. consigo.
2. yo
3. conmigo
4. tú
5. ti
6. contigo
7. mí
8. Ud.

Review Exercise Set 1-4

1. Julio lo lee.
2. Voy a estudiarla. La voy a estudiar.
3. Estoy escribiéndola. La estoy escribiendo.

Review Exercise Set 1-5

A.

1. Le escribo la carta a ella.
2. Él quiere darles el libro a ellos. Él les quiere dar el libro a ellas.
3. Él no está vendiéndole el coche a su novia. Él no le está vendiendo el coche a su novia.

B.

1. Me gusta Chile.
2. A él le gusta nadar.
3. No nos gustan las telenovelas.
4. Me gustas.
5. Me caes bien.

Review Exercise Set 1-6

1. Miguel se la muestra a ellos.
2. Raúl va a cantársela a ella. Raúl se la va a cantar a ella.
3. Estoy entregándoselos a ellos. Se los estoy entregando a ellos.

Review Exercise Set 1-7

1. Ellos se acuestan tarde.
2. Nos abrazamos el uno al otro. Nos abrazamos mutuamente.
3. Visto a mi niño.
4. Me visto a mí mismo.
5. Ellos se ven a sí mismos.

Review Exercise Set 1-8

A.
1. Se habla español aquí.
2. Se elige al presidente en noviembre.
3. Se venden coches aquí.

B.
1. Se dice que está aquí.
2. Se entra aquí.
3. Se sabe la verdad.

Review Exercise Set 1-9

1. Tengo mi cuaderno y ellos tienen el suyo.
   Tengo mi cuaderno y ellos tienen
   el de ellos.
2. Este libro es nuestro.
3. Mi familia vive en Venezuela y la suya vive
   en España. Mi familia vive en Venezuela y la
   de ella vive en España.
4. Mi hermana es rubia y la suya es morena.
   Mi hermana es rubia y la de ella
   es morena.

Review Exercise Set 1-10

1. Este cuento es más interesante que ése.
2. Aquella montaña es más alta que ésta.
3. ¡Esto es terrible!
4. Estos libros son fáciles y aquéllos son difí-
   ciles.
5. Esta casa es mía y ésa es de Pedro.

Review Exercise Set 1-11

1. Tengo la casa vieja y ella tiene la nueva.
2. Lo mío es tuyo.
3. La primera mujer es mi esposa y la segunda
   es de Marco.
4. Tengo doscientos libros, pero Pilar tiene
   trescientos.
5. ¿Ves a alguien?
6. No veo a nadie.
7. ¿Ves algo?
8. No veo nada.
9. Tengo varios.
10. Ellos leen muchas.

Review Exercise Set 1-12

1. Lo que
2. la cual
3. con quien
4. cuyo
5. que
6. las cuales
7. Quien

Answers to Section 2 (Prepositions)

CHAPTER 1

Exercise Set 1-1

1. Él llega a casa a tiempo.
2. Ellos ven a los niños.
3. Le mando el correo electrónico a mi hermana.
4. Al ver el accidente, llamé a la policía.
5. Ellos venden la fruta a cien pesos la libra.
6. Me levanto a las ocho.
7. Poco a poco, aprendo español.
8. Ellos van a la librería a menudo.

Exercise Set 1-2

1. Él habla español con acento extranjero.
2. Ellos van conmigo.
3. Sueño con mi esposa.
4. Él trae el trabajo consigo.
5. Estoy con mi abuela.
6. Ella tiene una cita con él mañana.
7. Ellos cuentan contigo.
8. Ellos llegan con prisa.

Exercise Set 1-3

1. Es el veintiocho de marzo.
2. El bolígrafo es de metal.
3. Mis parientes son de Bolivia.
4. Ella se cansa de estudiar las preposiciones.
5. Son las tres de la tarde.
6. Es el coche de Mario.
7. Él quiere una taza de café.
8. Aprendo las preposiciones de memoria.

Exercise Set 1-4

1. Pensamos en ir a la biblioteca.
2. Ellos viajan en tren.
3. En verano, nado mucho.
4. Tengo un examen en cuatro días.
5. Me fijo en la mujer.
6. Son las cinco en punto.

Exercise Set 1-5

1. de
2. Al
3. con
4. en
5. a
6. en
7. de
8. a
9. a
10. de

Exercise Set 1-6

1. Isabel está a la derecha de Bernardo.
2. Portugal está al oeste de España.
3. Los libros están al lado del escritorio.
4. Estamos cerca de la plaza central.
5. Al lado de la librería, hay un parque.
6. Ella está delante de la clase hoy.
7. La casa está dentro de la ciudad.
8. Enfrente de él está el estadio.

Exercise Set 1-7

1. A lo largo de la carretera, hay muchos sitios interesantes.
2. Debes ir más allá de las montañas.
3. Di un paseo alrededor de la plaza ayer.
4. Beatriz viaja hacia Barcelona.
5. Voy al campo a menudo.
6. Él corre por el parque.

Exercise Set 1-8

1. Como antes de ir a la oficina.
2. Me sentí enfermo/-a desde ayer.
3. Durante la tarde, bebo café.
4. Después de leer el periódico, voy a la oficina.
5. Voy a estudiar hasta las ocho.
6. Por la mañana, doy un paseo.

Exercise Set 1-9

1. según tú
2. incluso yo
3. excepto (menos, salvo) yo
4. entre él y yo
5. según Ud.
6. incluso nosotros

CHAPTER 2

Exercise Set 2-1

A.

1. Para la semana próxima, debo hacer esta tarea.
2. Para una adolescente, ella estudia mucho.
3. Esta copa para vino es mía.
4. Estos regalos son para Beatriz.
5. Parto para Salamanca mañana.
6. Para estar en Lima, debo partir temprano.
7. Para mí, es demasiado tarde.
8. Ella estudia para enfermera.
9. Tengo que estar allí para el viernes.
10. Vamos a comprar un coche para Enrique.
11. Este libro es para aprender los pronombres y las preposiciones.

B.

1. purpose
2. goal of an action or set of actions
3. personal opinion
4. final destination
5. personal opinion
6. time limit or specific point in time
7. purpose
8. comparison
9. personal opinion
10. final destination
11. suitability or ultimate purpose

Exercise Set 2-2

A.

1. Juan viaja por tren.
2. Ellos fueron por pizza.
3. Ella estaba por llorar.
4. Viajamos por avión.
5. Trabajas mucho por tu familia.
6. Por supuesto, puedo ir.
7. Pago tres dólares por litro.
8. Voy a ir por helado.
9. El libro fue vendido por el dependiente.
10. Él tiene much cariño por su esposa.

11. Quiero la tarea por escrito.
12. Por estar enfermo, no trabajé.

B.

1. idiomatic usage of **estar por** / *to be about to*
2. agent in passive voice
3. agent in passive voice
4. in exchange for
5. duration of time
6. emotion
7. multiplication
8. approximate location
9. means (transportation)
10. approximate location
11. substitution (in exchange for)
12. duration of time

Exercise Set 2-3

1. por. Idiomatic usage of **estar por** / *to be about to.*
2. para. Time limit.
3. para. Personal opinion.
4. por. Emotion.
5. por. Exchange.
6. por. Agent (passive voice).
7. por. Idiomatic or fixed expression.
8. para. Purpose.
9. por. Motivation.
10. para. Purpose.
11. por. Approximate location.
12. para. Purpose. por. Approximate location.

Exercise Set 2-4

1. Marina pasa por el parque. Approximate location.
2. Blas hace esto para su familia. Purpose.
3. Ernesto y Elena se hablan mucho por teléfono. Means.
4. Raquel paga diez euros por el libro. Exchange.
5. Eusebio usa tijeras para cortar el papel. Purpose.

Exercise Set 2-5

1. para. Destination.
2. para. Goal.
3. por. Approximate location.
4. por. Fixed expression.
5. para. Destination.
6. por. About to.
7. para. Purpose.
8. por. Means.

9. por. Exchange.
10. para. Time limit.
11. por. Approximate location. para. Purpose.

Exercise Set 2-6

1. para. Destination. por. Approximate location.
2. para. Personal opinion. por. Motivation.
3. para. Purpose. por. Motivation (*because of*).

CHAPTER 3

Exercise Set 3-1

1. Pido la cuenta.
2. Ellos sacan la basura.
3. Indicamos la tienda.
4. Pagas los libros con un cheque.
5. Ellos escuchan la música popular.
6. Ella enciende las luces por la noche.
7. Le agradezco los regalos a ella.
8. Él busca una novela.
9. Espero a mi novia.
10. Siempre miro la televisión.
11. Crío a mis niños.
12. Ellos apagan las luces.
13. Me quito la ropa.
14. Subo la escalera.
15. Logro hacer la tarea.
16. Espero el autobús.

Exercise Set 3-2

1. Vuelvo a Chile.
2. Vamos a México.
3. Ella se acostumbra a manejar.
4. Él llega a casa temprano.
5. Ud. se niega a escuchar.
6. Corres al parque.
7. Ellos aprenden a hablar español.
8. Subo a la montaña.
9. Me decido a leer.
10. Huele a flores.
11. Ella me enseña a escribir bien.
12. Mi hermana se parece a Madonna.
13. Animo a Carmen a leer más.
14. Ellos se apresuran a estudiar la lección.
15. La inspiramos a estudiar más.
16. Ellos llegan a Montevideo.

Exercise Set 3-3

1. Me enojo con mi amigo.
2. Ella sueña con Buenos Aires.
3. Él sale con Elena.
4. Ellos se asocian con gente importante.
5. Él tropieza con la silla.
6. Acabo con este trabajo.
7. Él se casa con ella.
8. Me divierto con mis amigos.
9. Ellos cumplen con la ley.
10. Llleno el vaso con leche.
11. Me asocio con gente simpática.
12. Me contento con la música.
13. Me conformo con las costumbres.
14. Cuento con mis amigos.
15. Me encaro con el enemigo.
16. Doy con mis padres.

Exercise Set 3-4

1. Esta carta sirve de recordatorio.
2. Ella se va de la biblioteca.
3. Ellos se quejan de todo.
4. Tratas de leer muchos libros.
5. Me muero de hambre.
6. Ella cesa de fumar.
7. Él se acuerda de su nombre ahora.
8. Me maravillo de su sabiduría.
9. El tiempo depende de la estación.
10. Me olvido de ir a casa a veces.
11. Ellos se libran de la basura.
12. Ella sale del edificio.
13. Ella se arrepiente de sus pecados.
14. Nos cansamos de estudiar las preposiciones.
15. Quiero cesar de fumar.
16. Depende del tiempo.

Exercise Set 3-5

1. Ella tarda en hacer el trabajo.
2. Persisto en leer el periódico.
3. Me confío en mi esposa.
4. Ellos insisten en ir a Barcelona.
5. Ella se fija en el coche.
6. Pensamos mucho en ir a la playa.
7. Él se ocupa del trabajo.
8. Ellos consienten en ir.
9. Él se complace en leer.
10. Ella persiste en cantar.
11. Me fijo en ella.
12. Uds. piensan en trabajar tarde.
13. Ellos se ocupan de sus parientes.
14. Insisto en ir.

Exercise Set 3-6

1. Me preocupo por el examen.
2. Ellos optan por viajar a Honduras.
3. Ella acaba por caminar a casa.
4. Ellos trabajan por la paz.
5. Él llora por todo.
6. Trabajo por el futuro de mi hijo.
7. Nos impacientamos por salir a tiempo.
8. Ellos se esfuerzan por llegar a tiempo.
9. Preguntas por el dinero.
10. Cambio dólares por pesos.
11. Abogo por mi cliente.
12. Nos esforzamos por estudiar más.
13. Mando el paquete por correo.
14. Ud. trabaja por su familia.
15. Estamos por esa mejora.
16. Ellos optan por menos trabajo.

Exercise Set 3-7

A.

1. Pilar acaba de leer este libro.
2. Vamos a ir a Montevideo.
3. Ella vuelve a leer ese capítulo.

B.

1. a
2. con
3. en
4. —
5. con
6. de
7. a
8. —
9. de
10. con
11. de
12. en
13. por
14. —
15. por
16. —

Exercise Set 3-8

1. Teresa está contenta con su familia.
2. Esta chaqueta es propia para Juan.
3. Isabel está acompañada de su marido.
4. Jorge es siempre el último en ir a casa.
5. El coche está cubierto de lodo.
6. Estamos libres de la deuda.
7. Estoy listo para salir.
8. Miguel es difícil de encontrar.
9. Es fácil de leer.

10. Ella es reponsable de llegar a tiempo.
11. Es difícil de estudiar aquí.
12. Alicia está dotada de mucho talento.

ANSWERS TO REVIEW OF SECTION 2 (PREPOSITIONS)

Review Exercise Set 1-1

A.

1. al, en
2. Al, a
3. a, con
4. En
5. de
6. Al
7. en
8. de
9. a
10. de

B.

1. al sur de
2. Antes de
3. Entre
4. hacia
5. contigo
6. A lo largo de
7. Hasta
8. a la derecha de
9. En lugar de
10. Según

Review Exercise Set 1-2

1. Para
2. por
3. Por
4. para
5. por
6. para
7. por
8. por

Review Exercise Set 1-3

1. a
2. con
3. de
4. en
5. por
6. de
7. de
8. —

English-Spanish Vocabulary

The vocabulary in this section will allow you to complete the exercises in this book. Note the following abbreviations: *m.* (= masculine), *f.* (= feminine), *n.* (= noun), *v.* (= verb), *sg.* (= singular), *pl.* (= plural).

A

... again (to)   **volver (ue) (a)** (+ *infinitive*)
a lot   **mucho** (*adverb*)
a lot of   **mucho/-a**
accent   **acento** (*m.*)
accident   **accidente** (*m.*)
accompanied by   **acompañado/-a (de)** (*n.*)
according to   **según** (*with subject pronoun*)
ache (to)   **doler (ue)**
actor   **actor** (*m.*)
address   **dirección** (*f.*)
admit (to)   **admitir**
adolescent   **adolescente** (*m., f.*)
affection   **cariño** (*m.*)
after (*time*)   **después de**
afternoon   **tarde** (*f.*)
all   **todo/-a/-os/-as**
along   **a lo largo de**
also   **también**
always   **siempre**
another   **otro/-a**
apartment   **apartamento** (*m.*)
appointment   **cita** (*f.*)
around   **alrededor de**
arrive (to)   **llegar (a)** (*v., n.*)
as for   **para**
ask for (to)   **pedir (i, i)**
assignment   **tarea** (*f.*)
associate with (to)   **asociarse (con)** (*n.*)
at   **a**
at eight   **a las ocho**
at eleven   **a las once**
at home   **en casa**
at night   **por la noche**
at times   **a veces**

B

battery charger   **cargador de pilas** (*m.*)
be (to)   **ser, estar** (*location*)
be about to (to)   **estar por**
be attracted to (to) (*people*)   **gustar**
be busy with (to)   **ocuparse (de)** (*v., n.*)
be enchanting to (to)   **encantar**
be enough (to)   **bastar**
be finished with (to)   **acabar (con)** (*n.*)
be going to (to)   **ir (a)** (+ *infinitive*)
be hot (to)   **hacer calor**
be important to (to)   **importar (a)**
be in favor of (to)   **estar por** (*v., n.*)
be inclined to (to)   **estar por**
be interesting to (to)   **interesar (a)**
be painful (to)   **doler (ue)**
be pleasing to (to)   **gustar (a)**
be sufficient (to)   **bastar**
be suitable (to)   **propio (para)** (*v., n.*)
be thankful for (to)   **agradecer (por)**
be tired of (to)   **cansarse (de)** (*v., n.*)
beach   **playa** (*f.*)
because of   **por**
become accustomed to (to)   **acostumbrarse (a)** (*v., n.*)
become impatient about (to)   **impacientarse (por)** (*v., n.*)
beer   **cerveza** (*f.*)
before (time)   **antes de**
beside   **al lado de**
better   **mejor**
between   **entre** (*with subject pronoun*)
beyond   **más allá de**
big   **grande**
bilingual   **bilingüe**
bill   **cuenta** (*f.*)
black   **negro/-a**
blond   **rubio/-a**
blue   **azul**
Bolivia   **Bolivia**
book   **libro** (*m.*)
bookstore   **librería** (*f.*)
both   **ambos/-as**

bother (to)   **molestar**
break (to)   **romper**
bring (to)   **traer**
bring up (to)   **criar**
broken   **roto/-a**
brother   **hermano** (*m.*)
brunette   **moreno/-a**
building   **edificio** (*m.*)
bump into (to)   **tropezar** (**ie**) (**con**) (*n.*)
bus   **autobús** (*m.*)
but   **pero**
buy (to)   **comprar**
by   **para**, **por** (*with true passive*) (see Section Two, Chapter 2)
by heart   **de memoria**
by mail   **por correo**
by plane   **por avión**
by telephone   **por teléfono**
by train   **por tren**, **en tren**

C

call (to)   **llamar**
can (*v.*)   **poder** (**ue**)
capital   **capital** (*f.*)
car   **coche** (*m.*)
cat   **gato** (*m.*)
CD   **disco compacto** (*m.*)
cell phone   **teléfono celular** (*m.*)
chair   **silla** (*f.*)
check   **cheque** (*m.*)
child   **niño** (*m.*), **niña** (*f.*)
Chile   **Chile**
city   **ciudad** (*f.*)
class   **clase** (*f.*)
clerk   **dependiente** (*m.*), **dependienta** (*f.*)
client   **cliente** (*m.*)
climb up (to)   **subir** (**a**) (*n.*)
close (to)   **cerrar** (**ie**)
clothes   **ropa** (*f.*)
coffee   **café** (*m.*)
color   **color** (*m.*)
come (to)   **venir** (**a**)
come upon (to)   **dar** (**con**) (*n.*)
complain about (to)   **quejarse** (**de**) (*v.*, *n.*)
comply with (to)   **cumplir** (**con**) (*n.*)
composition   **composición** (*f.*)
computer   **computadora** (*f.*)
confide in (to)   **confiar** (**en**) (*v.*, *n.*)
conform with (to)   **conformarse** (**con**) (*v.*, *n.*)
consent to (to)   **consentir** (**ie**, **i**) (**en**) (*v.*)

content oneself with (to)   **contentarse** (**con**) (*v.*, *n.*)
count on (to)   **contar** (**ue**) (**con**) (*n.*)
country   **campo** (*m.*) (*rural area*)
cousin   **primo** (*m.*), **prima** (*f.*)
cover (to)   **cubrir**
covered with   **cubierto/-a** (**de**) (*n.*)
cry about (to)   **llorar** (**por**) (*v.*, *n.*)
cup   **taza** (*f.*)
current   **actual**
custom   **costumbre** (*f.*)

D

dance (to)   **bailar**
date   **fecha** (*f.*)
daughter   **hija** (*f.*)
day   **día** (*m.*)
debt   **deuda** (*f.*)
decide (to)   **decidirse** (**a**) (*v.*)
delay (to)   **tardar** (**en**) (*v.*, *n.*)
depend on (to)   **depender** (**de**) (*v.*, *n.*)
desk   **escritorio** (*m.*)
die of (to)   **morir** (**ue**, **u**) (**de**) (*n.*)
difficult to   **difícil** (**de**) (*v.*)
discount   **descuento** (*m.*)
do (to)   **hacer**
doctor   **médico** (*m.*)
dog   **perro** (*m.*)
dollar   **dólar** (*m.*)
door   **puerta** (*f.*)
downtown   **centro** (*m.*)
dream about (to)   **soñar** (**ue**) (**con**) (*v.*, *n.*)
dress (to) (*someone*)   **vestir** (**i**, **i**)
drink (to)   **beber**
drive   **manejar**
during   **durante**

E

each other   **el uno al otro**, **unos a otros**
early   **temprano**
easy to   **fácil** (**de**) (*v.*)
eat (to)   **comer**
eight   **las ocho** (*time*)
eighth   **octavo/-a**
elect (to)   **elegir** (**i**, **i**)
eleven o'clock   **las once**
email   **correo electrónico** (*m.*)
embrace (to)   **abrazar**
encourage (to)   **animar** (**a**) (*v.*)
end up (to)   **acabar** (**por**) (*v.*)
endowed with   **dotado/-a** (*de*) (*n.*)

enemy **enemigo** (*m.*), **enemiga** (*f.*)
English **inglés** (*m.*)
enjoy oneself with (to) **divertirse** (**ie, i**) (**con**) (*n.*)
enter (to) **entrar** (**en**) (*n.*)
error **error** (*m.*)
euro **euro** (*m.*)
Eva's **de Eva**
every body **todos/-a**
every day **cada día**
every week **cada semana**
everything **todo/-a**
exam **examen** (*m.*)
except **excepto** (**salvo, menos**) (*with subject pronoun*)
exchange (to) **cambiar** (**por**) (*n.*)
exercise (to) **hacer ejercicio**
expensive **caro/-a**

F

face (to) **encararse** (**con**) (*n.*)
facing **enfrente de**
fall asleep (to) **dormirse** (**ue, u**)
family **familia** (*f.*)
famous **famoso/-a**
far away **lejos**
fear (to) **temer**
feel (to) **sentirse** (**ie, i**)
few **pocos/-as**
fifth **quinto/-a**
fill with (to) **llenar** (**con**) (*n.*)
film **película** (*f.*)
finish with (to) **acabar** (**con**) (*n.*)
first **primer(o)/-a**
fish **pescado** (*m.*)
five o'clock **las cinco**
five **cinco**
flamenco **flamenco** (*m.*)
flower **flor** (*f.*)
food **comida** (*f.*)
foolish **tonto/-a**
for **para, por** (see Section Two, Chapter 2)
foreign **extranjero/-a**
forget (to) **olvidarse** (**de**) (*v., n.*)
former **aquél/aquélla/-os/-as**
four **cuatro**
fourth **cuarto/-a**
free of **libre** (**de**) (*n.*)
frequently **frecuentemente**
Friday **viernes** (*m.*)
friend **amigo** (*m.*), **amiga** (*f.*)
from **de**

from the **del** (**de la, de los, de las**)
fruit **fruta** (*f.*)
future **futuro** (*m.*)

G

garbage **basura** (*f.*)
get angry with (to) **enojarse** (**con**) (*n.*)
get dressed (to) **vestirse** (**i, i**)
get married to (to) **casarse** (**con**) (*n.*)
get rid of (to) **librarse** (**de**) (*n.*)
get sick (to) **enfermarse**
get tired (to) **cansarse** (**de**) (*v., n.*)
get up (to) **levantarse**
gift **regalo** (*m.*)
girlfriend **novia** (*f.*)
give (to) **dar**
give a gift (to) **regalar**
go (to) **ir** (**a**)
go out with (to) **salir** (**con**) (*n.*)
go to bed (to) **acostarse** (**ue**)
go up (to) **subir**
good **bueno/-a**
granddaughter **nieta** (*f.*)
grandmother **abuela** (*f.*)
gray **gris**

H

hair **pelo** (*m.*)
hand over (to) **entregar**
happy **contento/-a**
happy with **contento/-a** (**con**) (*v., n.*)
hard **difícil** (*adjective*), **mucho** (*adverb*)
harder **más difícil**
hardworking **trabajador/-a**
hasten (to) **apresurarse** (**a**) (*v., n.*)
have (to) **tener**
have just (to) **acabar de** (+ *infinitive*)
have to (to) **tener que** (+ *infinitive*)
he **él**
headphones **auriculares** (*m., pl.*)
here **aquí**
highway **carretera** (*f.*)
home **casa** (*f.*)
house **casa** (*f.*)
hunger **hambre** (*f.*)
husband **marido** (*m.*)

I

I **yo**
ice cream **helado** (*m.*)

idea **idea** (*f.*)
important **importante**
improvement **mejora** (*f.*)
in a hurry **con prisa**
in front of **delante de**
in order to **para**
in writing **por escrito**
in **en**
include (to) **incluir**
including **incluso** (*with subject pronoun*)
inquire about (to) **preguntar** (**por**) (*n.*)
inside **dentro de**
insist on (to) **insistir** (**en**) (*v., n.*)
inspire (to) **inspirar** (**a**) (*v.*)
interesting **interesante**
invite (to) **invitar**
it **ello** (*subject pronoun, prepositional pronoun*)
it is eight **son las ocho**
it is hot **hace calor**
it is probable **es probable**
it is raining **llueve**
it is **está** (*location*), **son** (*with time expression*),
  es (*with adjective*)

J
jacket **chaqueta** (*f.*)
January **enero**
jewel **joya** (*f.*)
job **puesto** (*m.*), **trabajo** (*m.*)
July **julio**

K
kiss (to) **besar**
know (to) (*person*) **conocer**
know (to) (*fact*) **saber**

L
lack (to) **faltar**
language **lengua** (*f.*)
last to **último/-a** (**en**) (*v.*)
late **atrasado/-a** (*tardy, adjective*), **tarde**
  (*adverb*)
latter **éste, ésta/-os/-as**
law **ley** (*f.*)
learn (to) **aprender** (**a**) (*v.*)
leave **salir** (**de**) (*n.*), **irse**
leave (to) (*destination*) **partir**
less **menos**
lesson **lección** (*f.*)
letter **carta** (*f.*)

library **biblioteca** (*f.*)
light **luz** (*f.*)
like (to) **caer bien** (**a**) (*someone*), **gustar**
  (*things*)
listen to (to) **escuchar** (**a**)
liter **litro** (*m.*)
literature **literatura** (*f.*)
little by little **poco a poco**
live (to) **vivir**
look at (to) **mirar**
look for (to) **buscar**
lunch **almuerzo** (*m.*)

M
magazine **revista** (*f.*)
main **central**
make (to) **hacer**
man **hombre** (*m.*)
many **muchos/-as**
March **marzo**
Mario's **de Mario**
married **casado/-a**
marvel (to) **maravillarse** (**de**) (*n.*)
Mary's **de María**
meal **comida** (*f.*)
meat **carne** (*f.*)
metal **metal** (*m.*)
Mexican **mexicano/-a**
midnight **medianoche** (*f.*)
milk **leche** (*f.*)
mirror **espejo** (m.)
miss **señorita** (*f.*)
money **dinero** (*m.*)
month **mes** (*m.*)
more **más**
mountain **montaña** (*f.*)
movie **película** (*f.*)
Mr. **señor** (*m.*)
Mr. and Mrs. **señores** (*m. pl.*)
Mrs. **señora** (*f.*)
mud **lodo** (*m.*)
museum **museo** (*m.*)
music **música** (*f.*)
must **deber**
myself **a mí mismo/-a**

N
name **nombre** (*m.*)
near **cerca de**
nearby **cerca**
need (to) **necesitar**

neighbor   **vecino** (*m.*), **vecina** (*f.*)
new   **nuevo/-a**
newlyweds   **recién casados** (*m. pl.*)
news   **noticias** (*f., pl.*)
newspaper   **periódico** (*m.*)
next to   **al lado de**
next   **próximo/-a/-os/-as**
nice   **simpático/-a**
ninth   **noveno/-a**
no one   **nadie**
notebook   **cuaderno** (*m.*)
nothing   **nada**
notice (to)   **fijarse** (**en**) (*n.*)
novel   **novela** (*f.*)
November   **noviembre**
now   **ahora**
nurse   **enfermero** (*m.*) **enfermera** (*f.*)

O

of course   **por supuesto**
of the   **del** (**de la, de los, de las**)
of   **de**
office   **oficina** (*f.*)
often   **a menudo**
old   **viejo/-a**
on Mondays   **los lunes**
on time   **a tiempo**
on the right   **a la derecha**
one another   **el uno al otro**
one hundred   **cien**
one o'clock   **la una**
one   **un(o)/-a**
only   **sólo**
open (to)   **abrir**
open   **abierto/-a**
opt for (to)   **optar** (**por**) (*v., n.*)
organizer   **organizador** (*m.*)
other   **otro/-a/-os/-as**
ought   **debe**
ourselves (reflexive)   **a nosotros mismos**

P

P.M.   **de la tarde** (*afternoon*), **de la noche**
   (*evening*)
package   **paquete** (*m.*)
pager   **localizador** (*m.*)
parents   **padres** (*m., pl.*)
park   **parque** (*m.*)
part   **parte** (*f.*)
past   **pasado/-a/-os/-as**
pay for (to)   **pagar**

peace   **paz** (*f.*)
pen   **bolígrafo** (*m.*)
people   **gente** (*f.*)
persist in (to)   **persistir** (**en**) (*v., n.*)
person   **persona** (*f.*)
peso   **peso** (*m.*)
photo   **foto** (*f.*)
pizza   **pizza** (*f.*)
play (to) (*instrument*)   **tocar**
plaza   **plaza** (*f.*)
plead for (to)   **abogar** (**por**) (*n.*)
point out (to)   **indicar**
police   **policía** (*force*) (*f.*)
popular   **popular**
possible   **posible**
pound   **libra** (*f.*)
prefer (to)   **preferir** (**ie, i**)
preposition   **preposición** (*f.*)
president   **presidente** (*m.*), **presidenta** (*f.*)
prize   **premio**
probable   **probable**
problem   **problema** (*m.*)
produce (to)   **producir**
professor   **profesor** (*m.*), **profesora** (*f.*)
program   **programa** (*m.*)
pronoun   **pronombre** (*m.*)
publish (to)   **publicar**
put (*someone*) to bed (to)   **acostar** (**ue**)

R

rain (to)   **llover** (**ue**)
read (to)   **leer**
ready to   **pronto/-a** (**para**) (*v., n.*), **listo** (**para**)
   (*v., n.*)
receive (to)   **recibir**
recipe   **receta** (*f.*)
red   **rojo/-a/-os/-as**
redheaded   **pelirrojo/-a**
refuse (to)   **negarse** (**ie**) (**a**) (*v.*)
relative   **pariente** (*m.*)
remember (to)   **acordarse** (**ue**) (**de**), **recordar**
   (**ue**)
reminder   **recordatorio** (*m.*)
remote control   **control remoto** (*m.*)
repair (to)   **reparar**
repent (to)   **arrepentirse** (**ie, i**) (**de**) (*v., n.*)
report   **reporte** (*m.*)
resemble (to)   **parecerse** (**a**) (*n.*)
responsible for   **responsable** (**de**) (*v., n.*)
restaurant   **restaurante** (*m.*)
return (to)   **volver** (**ue**) (**a**) (*v., n.*)
run (to)   **correr** (**a**) (*v., n.*)

S

sacrifice **sacrificio** (*m.*)
sad **triste**
say (to) **decir** (**i**)
sea **mar** (*m.*)
season **estación** (*f.*)
seated **sentado/-a**
second **segundo/-a**
secret **secreto** (*m.*)
secretary **secretario** (*m.*), **secretaria** (*f.*)
see (to) **ver**
-self **mismo/-a**
sell (to) **vender**
-selves **mismos/-as**
send (to) **mandar**
September **septiembre**
serve as (to) **servir** (**i, i**) (**de**) (*n.*)
seventh **séptimo/-a**
several **varios/-as**
sharp (*time*) **en punto**
she **ella**
shirt **camisa** (*f.*)
short story **cuento** (*m.*)
should **debe, debería**
shout (to) **gritar**
show (to) **mostrar** (**ue**)
show how (to) **enseñar** (**a**) (*v.*)
shower (to) **ducharse**
sick **enfermo/-a**
sin **pecado** (*m.*)
since **desde**
sing (to) **cantar**
sister **hermana** (*f.*)
sit down (to) **sentarse** (**ie**)
site **sitio** (*m.*)
small **pequeño/-a**
smell (to) **oler** (**ue**) (**a**) (*n.*)
smoke (to) **fumar**
soap opera **telenovela** (*f.*)
some **algún(o)/a/-os/-as**
someone **alguien**
something **algo**
son **hijo** (*m.*)
song **canción** (*f.*)
Spain **España**
Spanish **español** (*m.*)
speak (to) **hablar**
stadium **estadio** (*m.*)
stop (to) **cesar** (**de**) (*v.*)
store **tienda** (*f.*)
street **calle** (*f.*)
strive to (to) **trabajar** (**por**) (*v., n.*)

student **estudiante** (*m., f.*)
study (to) **estudiar**
stupid **estúpido/-a**
suburbs **afueras** (*f. pl.*), **suburbios** (*m. pl.*)
succeed (to) **lograr**
suffer **sufrir**
suggestion **sugerencia** (*f.*)
suit one's interest (to) **convenir**
suitable for **propio/-a** (**para**) (*v., n.*)
summer **verano** (*m.*)
swim (to) **nadar**
symphony **sinfonía** (*f.*)

T

table **mesa** (*f.*)
taco **taco** (*m.*)
take a shower (to) **ducharse**
take a walk (to) **dar un paseo**
take off (to) (*clothing*) **quitarse**
take out (to) **sacar**
take pictures (to) **sacar fotos**
take pleasure in (to) **complacerse** (**en**)
   (*v., n.*)
talent **talento** (*m.*)
tall **alto/-a**
task **tarea** (*f.*)
tea **té** (*m.*)
teach (to) **enseñar**
telephone **teléfono** (*m.*)
television **televisión** (*f.*)
tell (to) (*a story*) **contar** (**ue**)
tell (to) **decir** (**i**)
terrible **terrible**
test **examen** (*m., sg.*), **exámenes** (*m. pl.*)
than **que**
that (*adjective, pronoun*) **ese/-a** (*nearby,*
   adjective), **ése, ésa** (*nearby, pronoun*)
that **que** (*relative pronoun*); **que** (*conjunction,*
   immediately preceded by a verbal expression)
that which **lo que, lo cual**
the fact is that **el hecho es que**
the **el** (*m. sg.*), **la** (*f. sg.*), **los** (*m. pl.*), **las**
   (*f. pl.*)
theater **teatro** (*m.*)
there are **hay** (*with following plural noun*)
there is **hay** (*with following singular noun*)
these (ones) **éstos** (*m. pl.*), **éstas** (*f. pl.*)
   (*pronoun*), **estos** (*m., pl.*), **estas** (*f. pl.*)
   (*adjective*)
they **ellos** (*m.*), **ellas** (*f.*)
they are **son, están** (*location*)
think about (to) **pensar** (**ie**) (**en**) (*v., n.*)

this **este** (*m.*), **esta** (*f.*) (*adjective*), **éste** (*m.*), **ésta** (*f.*) (*pronoun*)

those (*at a distance*) **aquel, aquella/-os/-as** (*adjective*), **aquél, aquélla/-os/-as** (*pronoun*)

those (*nearby*) **esos/-as** (*adjective*), **ésos/-as** (*pronoun*)

three hundred **trescientos/-as**

three P.M. **las tres** (**de la tarde**)

three **tres**

through **por**

ticket **boleto** (*m.*)

tire of (to) **cansarse** (**de**)

tired **cansado/-a**

to the **al** (**a la, a los, a las**)

to the left of **a la izquierda de**

to the right of **a la derecha de** (*preposition*), **a la derecha** (*adverb*)

to the west of **al oeste de**

today **hoy**

tomorrow **mañana**

too much **demasiado/-a** (*adjective*), **demasiado** (*adverb*)

too **demasiado**

tooth **diente** (*m.*)

toward **hacia**

toy **juguete** (*m.*)

traffic **tráfico** (*m.*)

travel (to) **viajar**

truth **verdad** (*f.*)

turn off (to) **apagar**

turn on (to) **encender** (**ie**)

twenty-eighth **veintiocho**

twenty **veinte**

two hundred **doscientos/-as**

two o'clock **las dos**

two **dos**

U

understand (to) **comprender**

university **universidad** (*f.*)

unpleasant **antipático/-a**

until **hasta**

upon **al** (+ *infinitive*)

useful **útil**

V

version **versión** (*f.*)

very **muy**

video game **videojuego** (*m.*)

W

wait for (to) **esperar**

wake up (to) (*someone*) **despertar** (**ie**)

wake up (to) **despertarse** (**ie**)

walk (to) **caminar**

want (to) **querer** (**ie**)

wash (to) (*someone*) **lavar**

wash oneself (to) **lavarse**

we **nosostros** (*m.*), **nosotras** (*f.*)

weather **tiempo** (*m.*)

week **semana** (*f.*)

well **bien**

what? **¿qué?** (*definition*), **¿cuál?** (*choice*)

which (one)? **¿cuál?** (*choice*)

which (ones)? **¿cuáles?** (*choice*)

who? **¿quién?** (*sg.*), **¿quiénes?** (*pl.*)

whom? **¿a quién?** (*sg.*), **¿a quiénes?** (*pl.*)

whose (*relative pronoun*) **cuyo/-a, -os/-as**

whose? **¿de quién?** (*sg.*), **¿de quiénes?** (*pl.*)

wife **esposa** (*f.*)

window **ventana** (*f.*)

wine cup **copa para vino** (*f.*)

wisdom **sabiduría** (*f.*)

with **con**

with him(self) **consigo**

with him, her, you (*sg., pl*), them **consigo**

with me **conmigo**

with you (*fam. sg.*) **contigo**

woman **mujer** (*f.*)

work (to) **trabajar**

work for (to) **trabajar** (**por**) (*v., n.*)

work **trabajo** (*m.*)

worry about (to) **preocuparse** (**por**) (*v., n.*)

write (to) **escribir**

Y

yellow **amarillo/-a**

yesterday **ayer**

you (*fam, pl., Latin America*) **Uds. (ustedes)**

you (*fam. pl., Spain*) **vosotros** (*m.*), **vosotras** (*f.*)

you (*fam. sg.*) **tú**

you (*pol. pl.*) **Uds. (ustedes, Vds.)**

you (*pol. sg.*) **Ud. (usted)**

your **tu** (*fam. sg.*)

yourself (*fam. sg.*) **a ti mismo/-a**